WOMEN *of* PURPOSE

WOMEN *of* PURPOSE

A DAILY DEVOTIONAL FOR DISCOVERING A MEANINGFUL LIFE IN CHRIST

SARA DAIGLE

Good Books

New York, New York

Good Books books may be purchased in bulk at special discounts for sales promotion, corporate gifts, fund-raising, or educational purposes. Special editions can also be created to specifications. For details, contact the Special Sales Department, Good Books, 307 West 36th Street, 11th Floor, New York, NY 10018 or info@skyhorsepublishing.com.

Good Books is an imprint of Skyhorse Publishing, Inc.®, a Delaware corporation.

Visit our website at www.goodbooks.com.

10 9 8 7 6 5 4 3 2 1

Library of Congress Cataloging-in-Publication Data is available on file.

Cover design by Jane Sheppard
Cover photo by Gautschi Photography

Print ISBN: 978-1-68099-341-7
Ebook ISBN: 978-1-68099-342-4

Printed in the United States of America

Day 1

"And the LORD went before them by day in a pillar of cloud to lead them along the way, and by night in a pillar of fire to give them light, that they might travel by day and by night." Exodus 13:21, ESV

I ran upstairs with a lump in my throat. Saying good-bye was never easy, but this time, the old farmhouse was even emptier than before.

Sibling number six had just gotten married, and her room was empty, still, lacking those two vibrant sisters of mine who always brightened my visits home. Living on the other side of the country made me wish everything stayed the same when I did get to make the long trip home.

But everything changes. Dad's beard was grayer, Mom's hair a bit whiter. They were talking of selling the house.

Gone would be the old wooden gate my brother built for Mom before he passed away. I thought giving him up was change enough, but life keeps moving at such a pace I wonder how the heart can keep up.

Home is different now. Two kids out of ten remain there, and the old home place may soon be sold to another family of ten, just like we used to be. Life is a swirl, a flurry, and even my own darling kids are growing at an alarming rate.

I can't hit "pause." On anything. Not even my own wrinkles, age, or youth. I keep growing older while the kids grow taller, needing me to buy shoes as large as or larger than my own.

This is freaky, scary business. Sometimes I want to bury my head under blankets while life speeds by. I mean, really, who ever thought I'd have a thirteen-year-old who is taller than her mama—and nowhere close to being done growing?

They eat, and they grow. That grocery cart in Costco holds enough to feed an army, and I grow silent when I see the bill. With four in tow and an overloaded cart, I get plenty of stares.

I'm proud of walking town with a ring on my finger and four lovely kids around me. Life is good, and I'm blessed. But this stage won't last forever. Soon, they will be teens, then be gone, and it will be my husband and I sitting in those chairs with graying hair and bones just a bit more brittle than before.

So why this dread of change? Isn't life all about change? Isn't change what makes the world go round?

Because if no one grew up and left the nest, no babies would be born. If no one grew old, the young would be left to navigate life alone. If there was no death of the seed planted in the ground, there could be no birth of new plants springing up. If leaves didn't grow brown and fall to the earth, new leaves wouldn't form in spring.

Life comes in stages, in phases, full of change, with nothing permanent. Even trials don't last forever, though we think they will. And each season is just that—a season that will soon be over.

Fruitfulness is a choice, not the happenstance of a certain phase of life. Fruitfulness comes when the heart is fixated on the Creator and making the most of each phase as it comes.

Let the kids be young, then let them grow. Let them sur-round you constantly, then let them leave more than you wish they would. Let yourself be called "Mama," then "Mom," by your growing son who wishes to appear manly.

There is nothing to fear. Not even old age, empty house, or growing kids approaching teen years. *"Perfect love casts out fear" (1 John 4:18, ESV), and He's come to bring abundant life that doesn't end when one season flows into the next before you catch your breath.*

You are born with purpose, created by a magnificent God, and you have no more say over your life than you did over your birth. He has a plan, a story to write, and He wants us to walk each chapter without turning away in mental avoidance of any season.

Each phase of life has His stamp of approval, His touch, His grace, His answers, and His deliverance.

We have only to hold His hand, and all of it becomes a story of grace, one more stroke of His brush over the canvas of our lives. He brushes beauty, He breathes grace when we fully live in each present He brings.

Life needn't be a merciless chase; it can be a flow of grace, a story unfolded, a learned rest that will lead us straight to the end with both purpose and peace.

We have only to find Him, walk with Him, delight in what He gives, and thank Him from the depths of our hearts for it. We have only to worship, to be thankful, to rejoice in the place we have in His story.

Because it remains that, at the end of it all, it really is His story, not ours. And because He's good, He wants to bless us at every turn of the road. *We have only to find those blessings and really live them up.*

Let the years unfold with all the changes they bring, because when the heart is set on Christ, *more years mean more wisdom,* and changes call for added dimensions of grace. The soul becomes rich, supple, amply supplied by tasting of it all.

We need fear no passing years, need dread no change, because embracing it all means being embraced by Christ.

Let such a Love lead us straight on with uplifted eyes, right into change without a hint of fear *because this life is meant to be power-filled by a powerful God, to be love-drenched by the Founder of Love, to be safely lived in Arms that know how to carry us right around the next turn of the road to our final destination.*

"Lord, teach us to make the most of each season, for each stage of life is ordained by you and is full of purpose."

DAY 2

"To one he gave five talents, to another two, to another one, to each according to his ability. Then he went away." Matthew 25:15, ESV

I watched her, this neat little lady teaching Protocol and Latin, and trembled a bit when my turn to teach came around. Truth be told, I'm just not as proper, researched, or knowledgeable as she.

We had joined a homeschool co-op for the first time, and I was navigating different waters, feeling out of the loop and unprepared. To top it off, my son appeared at the door as I was teaching to inform me that he had just locked all the keys in the car.

This time around, I didn't try unlocking it for two hours on my own. I dialed a number and soon the locksmith was on his way, this guy who rescued many people in their self-made mini crises every day. And as I watched him, it hit me once again, just how many people it takes to make the world go round.

We needed the learned lady teaching Latin, and we needed the locksmith. The mother doing science experiments trumped my own boring method of reading facts while trying to absorb the most important ones. My friend who organized and headed this class was indispensable, as was the lady who brought her gift of art to the classroom.

And later, I was struck with the simplicity of joy in the little ones as they played. They were free, happy, living up the moment in toy cars and trucks. They are such an important part of our world, just being themselves—not striving to be anyone or anything other than the children they are.

In the same way, we are an important part of God's world. See this? *God's world.*

There is the mail lady, the author of the books we read, the baker who creates the loaves my husband raves over, and the teacher who organized the class to begin with.

The humble in heart are satisfied to be a piece of the world, rather than believing the world revolves around them.

In His kingdom, there is no high or low, no striving to be what we aren't created to be, no boasting but to boast in Him and the cross.

There is no joy fuller than living out exactly what He's gifted us in without comparison to another.

No security greater than to dwell securely in the knowledge that He made us to be who we are, and is pleased with His creation.

There is no acceptance sweeter than knowing we are fully accepted by the Author of all things created.

No circle to be part of, but the circle of Love.

"Father, thank you that our purpose was preordained by you, for your pleasure."

DAY 3

"Arise, shine, for your light has come, and the glory of the Lord has risen upon you. For behold, darkness shall cover the earth, and thick darkness the peoples; but the Lord will arise upon you, and His glory will be seen upon you." Isaiah 60:1–2, ESV

The three oldest kids were gone when my husband and I sat down to dinner. When he asked how my day was, the brave face disappeared into my hands, and the eyes that had tried to hold it all in for the kids' sake welled up in tears nearly spilling onto the food in front of me.

"I've received horrible news for days now, and I'm not sure how to process it all. One friend just lost her son, another discovered four more tumors after already fighting cancer for four years, Hurricane Matthew threatens to devastate the island of Haiti, and the Syrian families are still brutalized by ISIS."

There we were, in our own cozy home with a delicious meal before us. But it didn't seem so long ago that it was us receiving sudden, tragic news.

I can still feel it, that gut-wrench inside when my brother disappeared under eighty feet of foreign water and stayed there for three days. Still picture my own dear mama riding those very waters in hopes her son's body would surface. Still see my father's face filled with unspeakable pain after dealing with the aftermath of his own son in the water for three days.

But I also remember something else. Those glory gates swinging wide for my brother seemed to swing wide for me, too, as we left the country and the plane lifted above clouds billowy and white. I knew it was a miracle that my heart felt just as soft as they appeared.

It was the miracle of grace.

This world is overloaded with tragedy, but we get to be overloaded with grace. When the heart breaks open, grace pours into the cracks, running deeper than if it had never broken at all. *We need not fear the broken, because it is an invitation to wholeness.*

When Job's children were killed, his livelihood taken, and his health gone to the wind, he sat and mourned, but he never cursed God as even his wife urged him to do. Somehow he knew there was a greater story going on than his own circumstances, and though he didn't know what it was, he trusted.

"Though He slay me, yet will I trust in Him" (Job 13:15, KJV).

If he could have known that God and Satan were having a discourse over one of God's most worthy servants, had he been aware that he was on trial before the powers of darkness as they did everything this side of heaven to remove his trust from his Father, he would have been even more faith-filled.

But he didn't know the full story.

Friends, our lives aren't the full story—*they are merely a part of the play in a great universe mastered by both light and darkness.* Don't let darkness deter your faith in the Light, because in the end, Light will triumph, and if you are to triumph with it, you must trust now before victory is full.

Either we allow darkness to overload us with the weight of it all, or we allow ourselves to be overloaded with grace because of, and in spite of, it all. We are on the winning side, and we get to bear a persona of hope, courage, and triumph as did those family members of the martyrs killed by ISIS when they forgave and expressed desire for their enemies to also know the light.

They saw the story, that light and darkness wage war. They chose to be free and bring others to freedom because they knew that only those overtaken with darkness would brutalize another. They know, and we know, that *"our struggle is not against flesh and blood, but against the rulers, against the authorities, against the powers of this dark world and against the spiritual forces of evil in the heavenly realms" (Ephesians 6:12 NIV).*

There are spiritual forces of evil, but see this? There are also heavenly realms!

We face loss and death and see the atrocities of evil all around us. Our enemy would bind our hearts with all of it so our eyes are blind to the Light. He knows what God knows, that light pierces darkness with rays so brilliant that darkness is dispelled.

You may live in a dark world, but remember this—Light pierces, Light dispels. Not only that, but Light shines even more brilliantly in darkness, and darkness must always give way because, though we are surrounded with it, it remains the lesser of two powers and will ultimately be cast down.

Lift your head today, allow light to flood your soul to its depths, and then, allow it to shine from your countenance and life in a dark world.

"Father, thank you that you've given us light greater than any darkness we may encounter."

DAY 4

"You prepare a table before me in the presence of my enemies; You anoint my head with oil; My cup overflows." Psalm 23:5, ESV

We all like to envision tables set before us, and most of the time, we think of a loaded table in an atmosphere of light and pleasantry. Overflowing cups and someone anointing our head seems to indicate a loving, safe, unusually grace-filled time.

But see this: *"in the presence of my enemies."*

This means when all is wrong and nothing's right and you want to sink into darkness because your world is heavy, shattered, and full of turmoil. When your enemies are still present, and their presence permeates your atmosphere and unsettles your heart and makes you want to cringe in fear or distress.

Here is where He prepares a table for you—*right here.*

Right in your enemies' presence, He wants you to sit and be fed. He wants them to see your feasting, and know you are a child well cared for. He wants others in your life to see His goodness to you in the face of impossible odds.

He's glorified in the dark, friends. We crave ease, but if all were ease we would not need a Savior and He wouldn't get to display His care in the presence of our enemies.

"Those who look to him are radiant; their faces are never covered with shame" (Psalm 34:5).

He says to you, friend who is in the trenches, friend who has a fatal illness, friend who doesn't know what to do with her past, friend who has discovered an unfaithful spouse, He says to you, right to your heart, that if you look to Him your face will be radiant, and you will not be ashamed.

You won't bow your head low in shame as you walk about town; *your heart will not wither, because He's preparing a feast to sustain you.*

He even has a trickle of oil for your head, just to let you know you are loved.

We mustn't be afraid of broken things. When the heart breaks open, it leaves a crack all the way to the core for Love to trickle in. If we were whole, competent, and satisfied, our hearts would not be as tender or receptive for the greatest Gift of all to saturate us all the way down.

That shattered place in your life that makes you want to cringe, run, or shut down—brave friend, will you embrace it today? Will you bravely say, "This is where I am, and God is right here with me?"

When you do that, Heaven comes to lead you right into the greatest grace you will ever know. *Embrace your broken, for in doing so you embrace Grace.* And that grace will prove to you a greater gift than if you were never shattered at all.

In that place, you become a testament of Love for the Love-Giver who so wanted the world to see how strong love is, that He sent His one and only son to walk among us, suffer, and die a cruel death in the hands of angry men—the very men He created.

He died, and then He rose gloriously. He wasn't afraid of

death because He knew He would rise. And you, friend, when you are no longer afraid of your own broken places, will rise with Him.

"Father, thank you for feeding us right in the presence of our enemies. Thank you that your love is known even more deeply when trouble surrounds us. Thank you that you triumph."

DAY 5

"Freely you have received." Matthew 10:8b, NIV

We drove away from the conference, us three ladies who had shared the car, the room, the table.

We shared lives, too, and deep places of our hearts, sitting there on the beds and floor with pajamas and pillows. But it wasn't until we drove home that she said it.

"Sara, you don't know how to receive from others." Her words hit me. She, who was constantly giving to me, was saying what? But I knew what she meant. I was more comfortable giving than I was receiving.

I had no problem serving others, but when they served me, I often felt uncomfortable. Like I was putting them out, and surely must be a pain in their side. I worked hard to love on others, but didn't want most others to sacrifice much to love on me.

It took many years to realize that God didn't need me to work hard for Him, either. He had already done what I could never do. My life changed when I quit trying and began trusting.

Do we really get this, that we will never be good enough for God? If we were, why would He send His Son to die a brutal death in sacrifice for our sins?

But do we also get this, that when we trust, His goodness is finally realized in our hearts and changes us from the inside out?

My journey of working to gain God's approval ended as I began trusting Him for His grace. My endless, exhausting efforts were replaced with *an immediate run for His arms when I felt sin rise in my heart.*

Where are we safer from our enemy's darts—on our own, fighting for all we have, or safely wrapped in Arms that hold it all, created it all, have it all? Which place guarantees more security? More victory?

We mistakenly struggle, strive, exhaust ourselves, when all God wants is for us to quit so He can begin. How can we realize His yoke is easy and His burden is light when we are running ourselves ragged trying to carry our own burdens?

And how, soul, will you ever receive gifts from others if you haven't yet received real sustaining grace for each and every day? *Your difficulty receiving gifts may indicate your lack of tasting grace you could never earn.* Because if you're performing to sustain friendships, are you possibly also trying to maintain your relationship with Christ by your own good works?

When you cease trying, He begins doing, and you never have to be afraid that He won't, *because He will.* When you allow yourself to be loved without performing for love, you end up drenched with love by Him who knows best what love is.

Be still. Know you are nothing, but He is everything. Know that, each and every day, you must not work hard for righteousness because He works mightily in you. And nothing changes your life as quickly as He does.

He breathes life into dead places.

He forgives when you can't stand yourself.

He gives victory freely when you cease trying to earn it.

His mercy is new each morning, even when your troubles are old.

His peace permeates and changes the churning spots of your heart.

His grace makes you new, washing away the hard and old to replace it with soft, fresh, waves of peace surpassing all understanding, all turmoil, all sin, all trial.

Allow yourself to be loved with such grace, given freely with no wages save that of His Son. From that loved place, allow those around you to give, sacrifice, and love hard on you.

You are treasured. You are loved. No matter where you've been, His plans for you stand and He wants to fill you with grace and joy, just as soon as you open yourself to Him.

"Lord, thank you that we cannot know true giving until we know how to receive your free gift. Help us to receive it, each and every day."

DAY 6

"Jesus answered them, 'It is not the healthy who need a doctor, but the sick.'" Luke 5:31, NIV

The soldier walked, limping, about the town he knew and loved before the war. How he wished the pain in his leg would cease.

Perhaps if he ignored it, it would heal in time. Daily, he re-washed and bandaged the wound. Each night, he applied cold compresses and elevated his feet. But nothing seemed to help, and months later he was still limping.

He had tried so many things, he didn't know what else to do. So he tried pretending. As long as a smile was on his face, no one would know about the wound on his leg or about the pain he felt with each step.

Living life pretending everything was OK seemed a better option than anything he'd tried before, so that's what he did.

Problem was, the wound never healed because he never did the right thing to heal it. He did what he thought would help, but it never really helped. Then, rather than stopping life in its tracks and doing whatever it took, he decided to perform as if it wasn't there at all.

The wound got worse with time, and before long he was in

bed, unable to move. Still smiling when others walked through his apartment, still pretending the pain was much less than it truly was. But after a while, when life became too painful, he called a taxi and made his way to the nearest hospital.

Finally, he realized he'd rather be dubbed as the "sick guy" who needed months of recuperation than spend the rest of his life with hidden pain. He'd even rather spend his life's savings to get well than be unwell with a full bank account. He was sick. And he was sicker now than he was at first.

Oh, soul. How many of us are the "sick guy?"

Do we forget that certain wounds need certain types of care? Pretending an infection isn't there just gives it a chance to get worse, to spread all the way to the bones, until your limb may need to be amputated. And if your limb is removed, your crippled life will affect not only you, but all those around you, and especially the ones you love most.

I'm not writing this to recommend different types of care; I'm writing this to encourage you to get care.

I know what it's like to hang on for years and then discover I'm about to go over the edge. I know what it's like to have tears right under the surface about the same old thing, and to pretend it doesn't bother me because I feel like others won't get it or I just don't know what to do with it.

I know what it's like to realize I'm going downhill instead of up, and to become more frightened with the slide down than of reaching out for help.

And then, I know what it's like to reach out and find healing, answers, love, and grace. I know what it's like to cry old tears from some deep place in my soul and for some wise person to know exactly what I need.

Someone saw clearly through the haze and reached into

18

depths I didn't even know existed. Someone handed me books to read that described my wounds, and yuck, even described who I was.

God used many people, places, and times to keep removing layers and *all I could do was say yes, and lean into it.*

We want it all fixed right away, or to pretend the wound doesn't exist. *Sometimes, we need to embrace our broken instead; need to lean into it; need to accept it fully, need to admit it's there. Always, before we find healing, we must cease to pretend it doesn't exist, and cease to care who knows it exists.*

We must want healing so desperately we no longer care if we land in the hospital and everyone knows we're there. We must quit expecting ourselves to be spiritual enough to know all the answers, and cease blaming ourselves for having trouble.

Rather than expecting one size to fit all, and berating ourselves for not being healed (especially if others think we should be), we need to look deeper, and allow those we know and trust to see straight into our hearts for what's really going on.

We are but one, and one person was never expected to know all the answers. It's just that we mistakenly believe we need to be a certain someone in order to belong, and be loved.

Do we know it's OK to be sick?

Owning your illness means you also search for a cure. But you will never look for a cure unless you first own your illness.

It's OK if few understand what's really going on in your heart. Find someone who does, and match their words to Jesus' words to see if they are suitable for healing. Whatever you do, don't pretend, don't go on, don't perform. There are always answers for your heart, and they are not contingent on others.

The gospel is personal, and comes to your own soul whether or not another receives it. And healing is one of the most blessed things about the gospel message.

Jesus came for those who are at the end of their own performance. He will do what we cannot do, give answers we cannot conjure on our own. Today, dare to say you are sick, then reach out and dare to apply the correct salve to prevent that wound from festering—and getting worse—with each passing day.

Then, dare to live whole and breathe deeply the delight of a soul at rest. You see the scar, but the wound is gone. *You are no longer defined by your wound, but by your healing.*

"Lord, thank you that in asking us to own our wounds, you do so that we may know your forgiveness and healing."

DAY 7

"And provide for those who grieve in Zion—to bestow on them a crown of beauty instead of ashes, the oil of joy instead of mourning, and a garment of praise instead of a spirit of despair. They will be called oaks of righteousness, a planting of the LORD for the display of his splendor." Isaiah 61:3, NIV

For the hundredth time, she took the shovel and scooped. Perhaps this time she would unearth something other than ashes. Something like rich, dark compost all mixed up to create the finest soil.

That's the kind of stuff all gardeners want. It's the kind of life all of us want. Somehow, we want the strange mix of our lives to decompose into something of great value.

But ashes aren't any good. And some things in life, no matter how long we scoop, remain ashes. We could go on for years trying to turn ashes into compost, but it just won't happen. Ashes are ashes are ashes.

We sit before the pile and stare at the hole we've dug, then give one last desperate attempt to turn those nasty flakes into something of worth. It doesn't happen.

That's how I felt one day as I walked the trails alone. Here, all is still, natural, quiet. The storm of my heart feels out of place and I want what nature is. "God, it just does what You created it to do. No questions."

Nature doesn't hurry; yet, because it is the art of God, everything is accomplished.

And He speaks to me, "You can, too. You can walk exactly how I created you to walk, to live, to be." I breathe it in. I know it's true. But it's such a journey, and I make mistakes as I go. I stumble hard, and sometimes I fall. So do those around me.

When I fall, I crash into them and hurt them. When they fall, I go backward and struggle to catch my breath.

I walked on. The sun set gloriously over the water and dusk settled on the trails.

I climbed up on a rock, and stood staring at the beauty of it all. Water swirled up the beach and washed sand around the rock on which I stood, safe and dry. I gazed at the foam, madly soaring up, crashing into the rock then down the beach, washing sand back into the deep.

But I stood on something that didn't move, and even remained intact despite the wildness around it. Ah, hasn't Jesus said He's our Rock?

Is it so terrible to have things we can't make sense of and have no idea how to fix? Is it really so bad, *when He holds out His hand to lift us to a solid place?*

I stood on the beach until the sun was gone, and I looked up into complete darkness. *The waves still crashed and swirled, sand was still swept away, but the Rock remained firm in light or darkness.* The trail was there, too, leading me into the trees toward the car.

I walked quickly, for the trail was dark and the woods deep. I glanced around furtively, and flipped on my flashlight and the beam splashed rays through the night, leading me safely to the car.

I didn't have all the answers, and my thoughts still swirled around just like the foam on the beach. But I had the Rock to stand on, safe and dry, and I had the Light to lead me through the night.

I wouldn't be able to handle the foam, but the Rock could.

I wasn't able to pierce the night with light, but my God could.

I could walk through night, and I could stay dry in swirling waters.

Hard things don't always mean you're in the wrong place; sometimes hard is the only way to get to the best place.

God doesn't always end the trial. You may expect Him to, because you pray and you do what you think you need to do. You may feel let down, disappointed, or even panicky when things remain right in front of your face.

Ashes are ashes and they remain ashes. But, when you stand on the Rock and walk in the light He promises to give, guess what? *He promises to give you a crown of beauty instead of ashes, because that's what God does.*

Sometimes those crowns of beauty don't come in the form we may wish. They may come in the silent hours of night as you talk with the Lord. They may be things of the heart that can only break forth from the fire.

Some people burn brighter and better from the fire; others are burnt up and devoured.

Climb up, flip on the light, hang on, walk patiently. That *thing* will not get the best of you, *because God has the better of it!*

"Lord, You promise to turn ashes into a thing of rare beauty. You promise to lead us into light. Help us simply to follow."

DAY 8

"Though the fig tree does not bud and there are no grapes on the vines, though the olive crop fails and the fields produce no food, though there are no sheep in the pen and no cattle in the stalls, yet I will rejoice in the Lord, I will be joyful in God my Savior.

"The Sovereign Lord is my strength; he makes my feet like the feet of a deer, he enables me to tread on the heights." Habakkuk 3:17–19, NIV

They told us not to be afraid of broken places, these two women who were interviewed on *Life Today*.

One had a cross penned on her wrist where she used to slice her skin with broken glass in a desperate attempt to get to the pain in her heart; the other voiced her recovery from the psychiatric ward where she occupied a padded cell to keep herself from harm.

Why are these two both listed in the top fifty women shaping Christianity today? One would never know by Sheila Walsh's bright smile, or by the fact that she has sold over four million books, written music, and recorded albums. And you certainly couldn't guess by Ann Voskamp's enthusiasm and excitement over the cross and "living given love," or by her remarkable success in publishing written truth.

The two lovely ladies seem to have two things in common: they are not afraid of their own broken places, and they are not afraid to share about those places to a broken world. They own their pain—and then, they own the victory miracle.

The couple who interviewed them also had their stories. An angry man turned gentle. In fact, more than gentle—he's a missionary and loves on a multitude of kids with his lovely wife. But that's not all; they've lost a daughter.

These four, so broken. So torn up. So down under in the muckiest trenches.

The fig tree wasn't budding, and there were no grapes on the vines.

The olive crops failed and the fields produced no food.

There were no sheep in the pen and no cattle in the stalls.

These influential people either lashed out in anger, mourned a daughter, cut themselves, or occupied a padded cell in a psychiatric ward. Do you see this? Is your life as bad, or worse? Or not as bad at all, but you still have your own empty stalls and fruitless vines?

They told us all the same thing: no one has to be afraid of their broken places. Your identity is not your brokenness, it is Christ. When we realize this, He makes us walk on high places. He's our strength, leading us to Himself in spite of our brokenness.

Make not your wounds your identity. Make not your success your identity. Make it Christ.

Did you know you can go from living broken to living love? Ann Voskamp spoke of the cross, how it's vertical, bringing love down to us; then horizontal, arms outstretched, giving love to the world around us.

Christ is always giving. If we allow our wounds, failures, or even successes to define us, we will always feel as though we are lacking something, that we're not living fully who we're intended to be. It's only when we allow our identity to rest fully in Christ that we will feel peace, rest, and fulfillment.

The words from the TV interview breathed life into my soul, and I knew I gave it all.

My wounds were healing, and I didn't need to be defined either by them or by success. I didn't need to accomplish things to be loved and worth something. I didn't need it—I really didn't need anything else to be valued.

These lovely ladies weren't worth something because they were successful. They saw redemption and their worth to Christ when they were in the trenches. They pulled out because they believed the love they felt. Then, God used them for Himself and the advancement of the kingdom.

None of it had to do with their own personal success.

My heart whispered one thing: Christ Jesus and Him crucified. Let Him be my all, not what I do. Let Him be my Source, my joy. Let grace be the defining factor permeating my soul until I reach those glory gates. With Christ as my identity, I have nothing to hold on to, nothing to grasp for.

I'm indebted to these two women who poured life words into my heart that day as I sprawled on the bed after a crazy morning with four kids who couldn't stop bickering. I'm eternally grateful to them for being vulnerable about their broken places.

I pick up my laptop and take a dare. I write of my lowest, most broken places to a friend who's walking the trenches. It's humiliating; it's scary. *But could it be that the cross holds more glory for the world when they see what it rescued us from?*

I pen it out, these inner battles of my soul, that time I wanted to hurt myself to get to the core of me that was so full of anguish, when I dreamed of being hit head-on by that semitruck barreling toward me, because the pressure in my heart made me want to crack open. What I needed was to allow love to pour into the broken places rather than create more empty brokenness. Breaking more wouldn't help; sealing up tightly wouldn't help, either. Only allowing love to pour through the open, broken cracks of my heart all the way to the innermost places healed my heart.

Perhaps if I share my broken places, others will know they are not alone. The cross I love to sing about will hold more weight, more glory. ***Because Christ, not me, is the good news.***

"Lord, thank you for being news more wonderful than any we could ever hear. Thank you for asking us to own our need for your grace. Help us to show our broken places with one another."

DAY 9

"And if I go and prepare a place for you, I will come again and will take you to myself, that where I am you may be also." John 14:1, ESV

Jesus gathers, invites, wants to live with us. His presence draws, includes, and embraces. Our enemy scatters, excludes, and rejects, but Christ embraces, holds, and pulls in with belonging. When we know Christ, we offer the same to others. We are not alone, therefore, we don't leave others alone. We don't want anyone left out of the encompassing love we know, and our lives are marked with including others.

Christ doesn't just say He will come and live with us (though He did that, too); He says He is going to prepare a place so we can live with Him. He wants us, friends. He wants to live with us.

Who do we invite, include, and cover with warmth and belonging? Are our own hearts closed up because we're afraid or feel unworthy, therefore shutting us out of the love and belonging that Christ offers?

We can't give belonging unless we first belong. We can't possibly invite others into our lives unless our hearts are opened by a large, magnificent love that can't be contained, can't be boxed in.

Belonging to God means you get to have others belong to your heart. The world over, those around you are hungry for love. We are born to be in a circle, not an empty box.

When we know the largeness of God's love, we find capacity to love large. Loving large means you approach others—your neighbor, your enemy, that rich friend, or that homeless woman—with love first and foremost. As God's love fills you, your heart will expand to love more people more deeply.

Breathe. Love large. Include all. Invite others.

"Father, if you hadn't included us, we would be lost.
Help us to reach beyond our comfort zone to the vulnerable
and weary, just as you did for us."

Day 10

"Behold, I have allotted to you as an inheritance for your tribes
those nations that remain, along with all the nations that I have
already cut off, from the Jordan to the great sea in the west.
  "The Lord your God will push them back before you and drive
them out of your sight. And you shall possess their land, just as the
Lord your God promised you." Joshua 23:4–5, ESV

I folded another load of laundry, and wondered at my restless
heart. Why did I feel so dissatisfied with the daily routine,
and why did I long for some deeper sense of fulfillment?

I sat across from my husband last night, and wondered
it aloud. "I feel so insignificant, so small, so useless. All I do
is teach school, prepare food, bring home the groceries." He
smiled, almost amused. To him, a homemaking, homeschooling mama's day isn't small or wasted.

But I wanted more. I wanted to feed refugees, and make a
great difference in a vast world of need. I wanted to heal the
sick and raise the dead and feed the homeless.

I want to love large, and my home seems small. But even
here, I'm having trouble loving large. *The little people I love
with all my heart, also take all my heart to love.*

I grab at the Word today, the day I've taught school again, took the twelve-year-old to get braces on her teeth, folded laundry, and fed the crowd one more time. I'm coming to God for my heart nourishment just as my kids came to me all day for their needs.

I see it here, *"I have allotted to you an inheritance"* (Joshua 23:4a, NAS).

Me, an inheritance. Me, the home-staying, homemaking, homeschooling mama who can't travel far or even write much these days because life swirls and the kids need and the Mr. arrives home from training, then leaves again for more.

While my sister travels to Africa with her brood to fulfill her life calling of bringing the gospel to the lost, I'm in a cozy house with my four kids. I'm at the gym with my husband. I'm talking life and love with him in the car. I'm washing dishes and grading worksheets and teaching little ones how to be kind.

The little kids I wanted to teach in addition to my own never came, because I saw I couldn't add more. I kick and buck hard, because I want to do more. But I believe, as I see it today, that *He's allotted an inheritance for me, right here.* The longing for fulfillment can be met in Him, and it's OK if it all seems small and insignificant.

Large accomplishments were never meant to satisfy the soul. The best of the best, after hitting the goal of his life, can still turn inward in dissatisfaction. The high of accomplishing lofty goals dims quickly and the heart turns to the next goal. We want the boost. We crave the rush. We want to dare, do, risk, and be rewarded.

Why did Marilyn Monroe design her own death after gaining the fame many of her fellow sisters long for? *The one who had it all, ended up knowing she had nothing.*

Jesus-loving, God-fearing women may not long for Hollywood fame, or even popularity. *But we may crave things other than Christ just as much, and for just as selfish reasons.*

The rush of accomplishment, the approval of those around us, the thrill of doing something brave. We trade loving Jesus for the love of ministry—and all for our own satisfaction.

Isn't this the case when we say we want to love large, but aren't loving well in the small world we do have?

Where is the lowly life lived by Jesus, Who didn't care about anything other than what His Father told Him to do? He was born in a manger; lived quietly for thirty years in a small town; never took kingship like He could have, because He was there for something even better.

If Jesus lived small with a love so large it conquered the world, can I also live small with vast love inhabiting crowded space, books, kids, and upside-down schedules?

Can I treasure these moments, knowing they make up the past, shape the present, and mold the future? Knowing that life is a marathon, not a sprint, and doing daily what helps me reach the finish line well is not a wasted life?

Contentment in living small means there's room for large love to inhabit me. And when large love dwells with me, He leads me to love, and it may be big or it may be small, and it really doesn't matter anymore, because Love just is.

In the secret, quiet place with Christ we learn to love large for reasons much greater than ourselves. We learn what an honor it is to simply be part of making God's universe go round, and we crave intimacy with the Maker of it all. From there, we let Him do what He wants with us.

Authentic intimacy begins in the heart, stays in the heart, grows in the heart, and best thrives in the quiet places where still waters run. He prepares a table for us in the presence of our enemies (Psalm 23:5).

Nothing takes His place, nothing satisfies more, and nothing opens your soul the way intimate love with the Author of it all does.

Rather than grasp for fulfillment in accomplishments, let's run for that quiet place and allow ourselves to be anointed. Let's stay in His presence and walk with Him. When we do, He leads us to the very places He has for us, and in those places, whether they are large or small, He has an inheritance allotted to each of us.

No soul who gives up her desire for accomplishment in exchange for intimacy will ever be disappointed. He will walk with you, right to the place He has for you. And you will find, to your surprise and delight, that your soul is fulfilled and your life purpose unfolds without you even grasping for it.

He leads you.

He unfolds for you.

He brings you to it.

He does it in you.

All you ever truly need is to know Him, and know Him deeply. From that place, follow the desires He places within you and live life to the utmost, for His glory. It's all about loving Him, being loved by Him, and sharing that love with the people He loves.

He may lead you to large places you never expected. Or, He may keep you in places that feel small.

Allow Him to go big with you, or allow Him to go small with you. Only make sure you are drenched in a large Love.

"Father, thank you that each of us have an inheritance, given by you, and we need nothing else."

Day 11

"I appeal to you therefore, brothers, by the mercies of God, to present your bodies as a living sacrifice, holy and acceptable to God, which is your spiritual worship." Romans 12:1, ESV

I stirred the large pot of chicken rice soup with anticipation. Today, the kids and I would be joining our friends to feed the homeless after church services.

One must wonder which is more of a service to the Lord—mingling with people who need Him most, need His love, His care, His tenderness—or sitting through another service of beautiful truth. Surely Christ served more than He was served. Today, though, I get to do both.

They trailed in, and I saw the face of the elderly gentleman who shared his life with me before. He didn't like the program provided in town because he didn't want the discipline. Even at his age, he didn't want the fresh start as much as he wanted to live easy.

My heart broke for him. I didn't return because I wanted to coddle him in his place—I returned because I know we all need grace in our weakness; we all need help; we all need Someone to lift us from the places we like to hang in.

We are loath to begin afresh because we don't see how much better we will be a year from now if we start today. We don't see that when God asks us to begin new, He wants to give us something much more valuable than the old we've had. *But we must begin.*

Healthy eating habits, though difficult to begin, may well increase both the span and quality of our lives. We may be loath to resist the foods we crave because we don't see ahead to the clear mind, healthy body, and rejuvenated spirit we will have a year from now, if we take the plunge.

God sees the result of saying yes; we may only see the denial and hard work. But we will never go wrong with a "yes" to God. We will grow old with apathy if we turn away from the new beginnings He offers to us.

We may begin fresh whether we are twenty years old, or seventy. God's heart for us stands whether we've dared follow Him or not, and taking fresh steps to the better refutes the enemy's plan to destroy us, no matter how young or old we are. Even if we're late, we honor God by choosing "yes." Beginning late is all the more reason to begin because we don't want Satan to have the final say in our lives.

In Christ, nothing is ever old.

Our bodies may grow old, but our inner selves are made new every single day. This is His heart toward us when He asks us to take a fresh start, away from the old into something new.

Let's follow Him with a "yes!"

"Lord, thank you that taking the dare to follow you
with a fresh start always leads to better things.
Help us plunge into new beginnings."

Day 12

*"'Because this people has transgressed my covenant that I com-
manded their fathers and have not obeyed my voice, I will no longer
drive out before them any of the nations that Joshua left when he
died, in order to test Israel by them, whether they will take care to
walk in the way of the Lord as their fathers did, or not.'" Judges
2:20a–22, ESV*

*"Now these are the nations that the Lord left, to test Israel by them,
that is, all in Israel who had not experienced all the wars in Canaan.
It was only in order that the generations of the people of Israel might
know war, to teach war to those who had not known it before."
Judges 3: 1–2, ESV*

Suffering friend, did you know that Christ Himself was perfected through suffering?

Do you know that your faith is made perfect through trial?

Do you read and see how Job was a perfect, blameless man,
yet was tested with the loss of all he had?

And do you see here, how God wanted the nations to know
how to fight, and He knew it wouldn't happen in an atmosphere of peace?

The first way through your trial is to embrace it. Own it. Don't run from it. Own your pain, then own your healing.

The second thing is to believe that God can use all things—not just some things—for your good.

The third is to know that you are on trial, and that many fall away because of trial. If you stand firm, your faith becomes stronger, not weaker.

The fourth thing to embrace is suffering. If Christ suffered, why not we? *We were never promised ease; we were promised grace.*

There will be "nations" the Lord leaves in your life, but by these nations you will become strong; *learn not to fear them, but to conquer them.*

We don't always suffer because of our own failure. We may be on trial for the glory of God, as Job was. And when God's glory is revealed through our lives, His glory is made known to our souls.

Because we are on earth rather than heaven, not all things will be perfected in our lives. We gain more when we cease trying to perfect all things and learn instead to know the Perfect One.

Defining our well-being by external things gives us a faulty, shaky foundation and leaves us empty much of the time. *We become occupied with grabbing at dust from the sky to fill our hands when Christ wants them to hold the Ultimate Gift in stillness and rest.*

Rather than grab at perfection and external peace for our well-being, we must hold on tightly to the One Being where all is well.

Responding to His positive input in our lives is much more productive than reacting to or trying to avoid all negative things. *When we are busy reacting, we have less time for re-*

sponding. Responding to good keeps us occupied mentally so there is less room for reacting to negative.

> "Lord, help us not to go down in discouragement, but to remember that each trial remaining in our lives is intended for our growth. Thank you that we are not destroyed, but grow instead."

DAY 13

"On the third day there was a wedding in Cana of Galilee, and the mother of Jesus was there. Now both Jesus and His disciples were invited to the wedding. And when they ran out of wine, the mother of Jesus said to Him, 'They have no wine.'

"Jesus said to her, 'Woman, what does your concern have to do with Me? My hour has not yet come.'

"His mother said to the servants, 'Whatever He says to you, do it.'" John 2:1–5, NKJV

I poured my coffee and held the warm cup to my cheek. Eyes lifted to the sky, my thoughts pondered the conversations I'd had with several women I loved and cared about. Life and love, death and love, living and love, are always mysteries to learn of.

There's no end to love. And I've had women ask me, "How do I love better? How do I love whole?" Their hearts have been broken and life has thrown unexpected curveballs, leaving them breathless in the search of what to do and how to do it, and how to have that love they long for, that every human being longs for.

Love's a mystery. Love takes risk. What if you love someone and they don't love you back, what if they love you but you don't love them? What if neither of you love each other anymore, and you both rise to another stoic, soiled day because the soul grows grim when love goes dim?

Being in love induces a rush of endorphins. You know zest for life, you care, no mountain is too great to climb and no valley too deep to walk. You feel powerful and power-filled. But what about those who've long lost that kind of love, or have never had it? What then?

Learning to love again, or finding love for the first time, takes risk. *But you don't grow anything without giving something.* And if your relationship is in the trenches—even if it has *always* been—love is especially risky. To love is to be vulnerable, and it is much easier to be vulnerable in an atmosphere of safety.

You may try to keep yourself together by closing your broken heart, or you may leave it open for love to fill the cracks all the way down to the core. Allow it to seep into the hardened walls of your heart, to penetrate your soul, to warm you all the way through, until that warmth is felt by your spouse. Own your brokenness, then set out to find True Love. Allow Him to pull layers from your hiding soul until you no longer hide.

Allow Him to break the sun forth on your face until you can't help but smile, not because your relationship is healed, but because your heart is healed.

Did you know your heart's healing won't come from your healed relationship as much as it will come from your Healing Savior? Your relationship won't heal until you let it go so you can cling to the Healer. You can't hold on to your spouse with both hands until you first hang on to Christ with both hands.

When you hang on to the Healer with both hands, and your spouse does as well, both of you will learn to love each other from the place of being loved. Hold on to your Savior with both hands so you and your spouse can heal both of your hearts.

And if you alone hang on, you will be able to show your spouse what love looks like. Rare is the person who will not respond to long, unfailing, unconditional love.

Hurting soul, you may wonder if love will ever come your way. You may wonder why you feel it gone, or even why you've never felt it. May I assure you, whatever your place, that Christ will take you to know the love He wants you to know? He will lead your heart to the place you long for it to be. The love He will work in you is worth more than the love you grasp for.

When the Mother of Jesus found herself in a wedding where the wine had disappeared, she looked for a solution. Somehow, though she didn't know how, she knew Jesus would remedy the problem and all she could say was, "Whatever He says to you, do it."

Christ won't lead you away from your spouse; He will lead you toward them. (Unless, of course, there are drastic things your spouse refuses to address and change. In such a case, leaving may be necessary for your own safety and well-being.)

Christ doesn't leave wounds unhealed; He heals them and even makes you better from them.

Christ never leaves you stranded; He promises life for your heart and joy to your days.

Hurting friend. You, the one with tears streaming down your cheeks at night. You, the one who sighs with longing when you see others with the love you desire.

You, the one who has lost her love, or you, the one who has never found it. Do you know assuredly that Christ will heal your heart and cause the love He has for you to win? That it is

His heart to accomplish His love, regardless of your hang-ups and failures? That His will is to fill your days with joy?

Only make sure you stay in His will, and whatever He says to you, do it. *You can't go wrong when you stay in the right place.*

Don't veer from it. Because trying to find the right kind of love in the wrong place will surely cheat you of the blessing He has for you. *Mary had a dilemma; so do you. Mary went straight to Jesus and the servants did as they were told; so can you.*

When Christ worked His miracle, the vessels were filled with wine better than the previously made wine. So your love, when it's grown by the Founder of Love, can be better than anything you dared hope for.

The question remains, will you allow love to grow and fully mature in your heart when that is God's intent?

"Lord, thank you that even a broken heart won't stop your love. Thank you that broken hearts better absorb your love, and are made whole."

Day 14

"But God chose what is foolish in the world to shame the wise; God chose what is weak in the world to shame the strong; God chose what is low and despised in the world, even things that are not, to bring to nothing things that are, so that no human being might boast in the presence of God . . .

"Therefore, as it is written, let the one who boasts, boast in the Lord." 1 Corinthians 1:28, 29, and 31, NAS

I held the child on my lap and looked into the eyes of the other three. How to fully express what was on my heart, how God doesn't think as the world does, judge as the world judges, or value what the world values? How to help them want Jesus's thoughts more than their peers' approval? How to help them see the beauty of weakness made strong with inner strength unknown to man apart from a miraculous rebirth?

I struggle to put it into words. The things of God are foolish to man, unknown to the natural. But I try. Their sleepy eyes grab at me, and I want them to know, young, what took me so long to grasp.

I pray over them, and the day is done. The next morning, I ponder these verses again, along with what a friend and I were discussing a few days ago. "I want to make a difference," she had said. "I need to start pursuing my goals somehow, however small it may be."

The brown-eyed, dimple-cheeked daughter asks me, "Mama, is it wrong to want to be a famous dancer?" She's a thing of beauty, born to dance. I struggle again to put into words what I think God's heart is for His people. "When God gifts you with something, it is honoring to Him when you cultivate and enjoy that gift, dear."

She nods. "We can dance for God, or run for God as Eric Lidell did." But Eric's chief desire was not for fame. When he ran, he sensed the gift God had given Him, and He knew the pleasure of His Creator as he sped along the track leaving others in the dust. When running opposed any other purpose God brought his way, he let go of it regardless of the diminishing attention. He left a world of fame to be a missionary.

Always and everywhere, He brought Christ's love to people. In this way, He boasted only in the Lord even as he crossed the country with fame to his name.

Knowing you are God's allows you to experience either lowliness or fame, while still boasting only in the Lord. When the heart is free, it is free indeed! The key is not to seek the fame, but to seek the Lord. Then, out of love for Him and passion for life, to do our very best with what He's gifted us in.

Better to have one multiplied gift than to have ten dormant gifts.

I meet with the lady who mentors me, and I share my life—the good, the bad, the ugly. And when I write that letter to another friend because I sense she needs to know my mess, my humanness, my battles, so she can know she's not alone, I'm stripped even more.

God, what does it mean to boast only in the Lord? I cringe

when I realize that sometimes even my devotional time is just a way to feel like I'm being a "good Christian." He shows me how low this is, and how I need only feel good about His goodness—not my own. *I become willing to exchange my goodness for His, and to exchange my own works for true love.*

Do we love because we truly love, or because we love to appear as someone who loves? Who are we, really? *Are we the good news, or is Jesus Christ the good news?*

The mower breaks again, and I shove it into the minivan one more time. The door won't shut, and I push, adjust, and mutter about old mowers and minivans. Nothing to boast of here. The van was dented and the mower broken, and I felt just as broken about myself. Because try as I did, I still hadn't figured out this heart of mine, and all I could do was bow before a good and wise Savior to ask for mercy.

And why did I ever think I needed to have some image of perfection when I'm so utterly far from any kind of goodness, apart from Christ?

I'm unloading the mower at the repair shop when the mechanic walks out. Frustration with the silly old mower dissipates into compassion as I watch him. He has no pride and treats me with shy respect, as if he expects nothing in return. I drive away and I say it aloud, "That man was one of the kindest, most humble men I've ever met."

He was boasting in nothing. I loved the resulting grace pouring from his weathered person. And I knew, just as surely, that I have nothing to boast of.

True reverence for the Lord is when we no longer use His name for our own agenda, but honor it so much we dare not use it to promote ourselves.

If we remain there, friends, with nothing to boast in except the Lord, *we become a magnet for grace.*

We receive mercy, and show it.

We live fully, right where we are.

We know we are owed nothing; rather, we are recipients of unmerited favor.

We live vulnerably, openly, humbly. There is no persona to uphold because we know there's no goodness apart from Christ.

Others can tell whether we know we are nothing, or think we are something. Our hearts affect our demeanor, our attitude, the vibes we spread into the atmosphere around us. Ironically, those who know they are nothing apart from Christ place themselves directly in the pathway of greatest blessing.

When you know you are nothing, Christ waits to bless your heart with everything. Not everything you wish for, but everything He wishes for you.

He's looking for you, friend who is stripped of all pride. You are in a good place, because God is watching to bless those who will give Him all glory, and be fruitful without becoming prideful.

Allow your heart's posture to be so taken with Christ that it cannot be absorbed with itself.

"Lord, thank you that the resulting grace from a humble person ministers to us more than perfection."

DAY 15

"Not that I have already obtained all this, or have already been perfected, but I press on to take hold of that for which Christ Jesus took hold of me. I do not consider myself yet to have laid hold of it. But one thing I do: forgetting what is behind and straining toward what is ahead.

"I press on toward the goal to win the prize of God's heavenly calling in Christ Jesus." Philippians 3:12–14, Berean Study Bible

In 1667, a Jesuit priest braved the Ecuadorian jungle to reach the unreached. He was murdered in an isolated station by the Auca Indians, the very people he had come to love.

As a result, white men ignored the tribe for nearly two hundred years. Around 1875, rubber hunters entered the area, and for the next nearly fifty years, the indigenous people were victims of brutal rape, torture, and slavery.

Is it any wonder that when Jim Elliot and his fellow missionaries entered the forbidden, hostile jungle, the threat of death loomed large before them?

Would it be possible for these natives to unlearn what was entrenched in their minds from birth—that white men were brutal creatures to be feared greatly? How much proof would be needed? How much time? And what sacrifice would need to be made to bridge the gap of centuries-old hostility and fear?

Jim Elliot gave his life, and then his widowed wife braved the jungle to live with the very people who had speared her husband to death.

Sacrifice. Death given in exchange for life. Gigantic steps taken to undo damage and give the heart another chance at love.

The Indians responded to love, and a church was formed.

Fear gave way to peace, warmth replaced cold walls of hearts.

Smiles wreathed faces where scowls had once been.

And the age-old fear of being speared to death by each other, then eaten in glee, was replaced with love and forgiveness.

If they could learn trust for the first time, could break down generations of bondage with the power of the gospel, what can we break out of? What do we need, desperately need, to replace in our hearts? And how much sacrifice are we willing to endure, how much effort are we willing to show, to bring life in place of death?

People are worth it, even though sometimes it may take years. Sometimes, we give sacrificially and never see a change. But are we willing to give, still?

Surely our fear is of the same spirit as theirs. We may not go hunt our neighbors, behead strangers for the safety of our tribe, or string the bones of our enemies onto our loincloths. But what eats at us? And what makes us so afraid? What kind of thing lurks in the recesses of our souls, casting shadows over our lives?

Do we rest assured there is a way out, that we don't need to live forever with our own darkness? As Jim gave his life willingly to show the native people a way out of their darkness, so

Christ gave His life for you, willingly, to bring you out of every single bondage.

Do you see that? *Every single bondage. Because nothing can hold you that can't be broken by the God who holds everything.*

Shackles fall to the ground in a mighty crumble.

Light appears in the eyes where there was once fear and insecurity.

Heaviness exchanged for lightness and freedom.

He came to bring us *that,* and nothing less than that. God's people are in God's shelter. God's people are given His gifts. God's people, of all people, have reason to live freely, to taste joy.

It passes understanding. When you have no reason to live joy, He gives you all reason to live joy. When the storm rages around you, even within you, He holds you in calm. You can't explain it because there's no earthly reason to feel it. *And the things that have always bitten you, have always made you squirm, have always destroyed your peace—well, those things are swept away by the power of the cross.*

The death of Christ was a much greater sacrifice than the death of Jim Elliot. Jim came to share the good news that Christ spoke of. Whoever receives this good news receives every promise of things made new, no matter how old.

Christ offers freedom. You may forget the old and be utterly taken with the new. *Friends, being taken with the new takes your breath away, where once the old took your peace away.*

*"Lord, thank you that we get to put the old away
and be taken with the new. We get to drop weights
and absorb the new no matter how old our shackles are."*

Day 16

"*One man among a thousand I have found, but a woman among all these I have not found.*" *Ecclesiastes 7:28b, ESV*

Thanksgiving week is over, and with it comes the tiredness of a holiday well lived. We cleaned house and made pies, mashed sweet potatoes and covered them in the gooey crunchy goodness.

I ask my husband if I should make the orange superfood a bit healthier this year, and eliminate the topping. His eyes grow large and he asks, "Is that even a question?!" I smile and head straight for the brown sugar. A holiday is a holiday, after all.

Guests arrive and leave, then weekend guests enter the door. Pumpkins get tossed and the tree is set up, the entire house aglow with lights. Rain pours on green grass, and we escape it to head into snowy mountains for an afternoon of white wonder with the seven kids. And by the time night comes along, I'm reaching for those earplugs with that desperate ache for sleep the body knows when life has been well lived for days in a row.

I stuff them in. Don't let me hear a sound, because I'm a light sleeper. Don't wake me, or I may be tossing for two hours straight, trying to get back to sleep.

And then I ponder, "What do I drown out that God is trying to say?"

Do we shut down the hearing of our hearts when that whisper comes? Ignore it, leave it for later, or tune out altogether? We may not live in blatant denial of Christ, but do we realize the apathy of soul that comes from ignoring the voice of the Spirit?

We may ignore the living voice of God in exchange for the dead desires of ourselves—then wonder why we're not fully living.

I may try as hard as I want to drown out noise from the house, but if I drown out God's voice, I lose. We may lose sleep if we don't plug our ears, but we will never lose life by unplugging our hearts and really listening in. We may grow weary if we don't get our sleep, but we will grow alive if we listen in on God 24/7.

Listening constantly helps the soul avoid those disastrous sinkholes, those difficult lessons that come when you plug your heart and do what you want, instead of what God wants.

Live with hearts unplugged.

My husband snores, and I nudge him onto his side, stuffing the earplugs deeper. But when God speaks to me in the morning, I want to listen well. Who knows the blessing He may have in store?

Who doesn't want an unbroken heaven; who doesn't want to be a magnet for grace?

I believe Mary was chosen to be Jesus' mother because her life was pure. See this, constant listening to Christ can only add blessing to your life. Was her path easy? Being with child while unmarried was a heinous thing in those days, but because she listened well to the Spirit of God, she had faith to follow through even to the time of her Son's cruel death.

Mary's heart was unplugged. God looked for a woman like this, and He saw her. He's still looking today; allow Him to see the same posture when He sees you.

Live unplugged. Tune in 24/7.

*"Lord, help us to listen in for the
One Voice more important than all the rest."*

Day 17

*"Let us then approach God's throne of grace with confidence, so that
we may receive mercy and find grace to help us in time of need."*
Hebrews 4:16, NIV

Tonight I poured wine, lit candles, and laid a tasty dinner
onto an attractively set table. My husband chatted with
the kids and ended up talking with them for a few hours about
things important to their hearts. Then, he played with them
while I showered and relaxed.

Nights like this are rare in our cop family world. Many
nights, we are apart, Daddy working the roads or gone on
training. Often Sundays are the same, and even some holidays
find him pulling over cars instead of enjoying a cozy home. But
tonight all is near perfect.

My day, though, was anything but perfect.

It had begun with a dramatic daughter overreacting and
yelling at all her siblings. It continued with her panicking when
she was to do her presentation in class, still learning that public
speaking isn't all that terrible.

By the time I was home, I was in tears. I admit it—I felt
battered and bruised over something relatively small, but it felt
like a lot.

As I lay there, I realized that even though I felt terrible about the day, I also felt incredibly loved by the Lord. How He loves with so much patience and mercy blows me away. I felt held and passionately loved by Christ. His love covered me like a blanket; His grace always surpasses any other grace I've known.

If my troubles were this small, how much do others hurt who have trials of much greater magnitude? And how many need love to see that their hearts hurt greatly even when their troubles appear small, like mine did today?

When you show people God's love, you draw them to God's heart.

Her words were like music to my ears, "It was a pleasure working with you today, a pleasure in every way." The mother who taught little ones with me spoke softly as she left. I hang on to her words because today, I need them.

If Christ loves me so warmly even when I mess up, how can I love others when they mess up? How can I look beyond the mistake right into the heart, and sit beside the soul who's already feeling beat down and knows she made a mistake?

How can I live given love to someone who feels deserving of none?

Just like He loves me.

I lit more candles and bright flames shed warmth to my heart. The happy face of my daughter's friend shed light all over the room. Just as small things bring comfort and light to our days, so small acts of love can bring great grace to someone's heart. *Never underestimate the powerful effect of small acts of given love.*

Live given love, just as you are loved by a Given Savior.

His mercy is so vast it covers me when I'm least deserving of it. His forgiveness is extended the moment I ask for it. When

Christ was on earth, He showed the greatest extensions of mercy to the woman caught in adultery and to the tax collector beating his own chest and saying, "God, be merciful to me, a sinner."

He revealed Himself in unusual frankness to the woman at the well, who knew she was a sinner, having had five husbands and now living with a man she wasn't married to. Everywhere, He seemed to show lavish love to the ones who knew they were in need.

How is it, then, that those around us who are in need of repair get less mercy than those who are pleasant and near perfect to hang out with? How is it that we serve a God of such extravagant patience, yet readily shoot arrows when someone falls, or even makes a mistake?

The longer I live, the fewer arrows I shoot. God knows how many undeserved buckets of grace I've received and still need to receive. God knows the mistakes I make with friends and family, yet still desire their love and grace.

God knows why He extended lavish amounts of grace to people with guilty heads bowed low, but gave little to those who shot jealous, self-righteous arrows at His very Godhead because they were so prideful they couldn't even see when they loved themselves more than the God they professed to serve.

Some people say unbelievers are more transparent, honest, real, and loving than many Christians. Could it be because Christians often uphold an unrealistic persona of perfection, more for our own honor than for the honor of Christ?

Next time that person in your life is a mess, or makes a mistake, can you look him in the eye to gain access to his soul rather than to let him see your disapproval?

Live given love. Love purposefully on the broken, the ones who are having a bad day. Listen well, then love well.

Today, hold a hand.

Today, buy a coffee for a loved one.

Today, give lavish praise. Compliment someone on that new sweater or beautiful hair. Give it freely.

Today, place your phone out of reach so you can gaze into the eyes of your child more than into the face of some friend hundreds of miles away.

Today, choose to give that $20 when you could turn away.

As freely as you've received love, so give it freely away. As much as you were pursued in your sin, so sit down to understand, ask, and pursue that person in your life.

Love well, and you will live well. Love hard, and you will bring light and life to many hearts who need to see beyond the darkness of their lives.

"Lord, help us to give love forward today."

DAY 18

"There is no fear in love, but perfect love casts out fear, because fear has torment." 1 John 4:18a, ESV

This afternoon found me surrounded with Christmas gifts to wrap, cards to address and mail, music to play, and fudge to make. It's only December 4, but I can't wait. This month will be festive, because celebrations are a joy—especially celebrating the One who came to save us from the monster of fear.

Have you ever had panic attacks? I remember lying on my bed as a young girl, trying to rest but my heart pounding as hard as if I had just run a mile. I remember staring at my acne-ridden face, knowing the stress of fear caused my normally clear skin to break out violently.

What was I so afraid of?

I remember living with fear of death, and life, and everything in between. Some days I felt I would be safer if I just buried myself in the covers of my bed and stayed there. I was afraid of people, afraid of myself, afraid of God, and I never, ever felt good enough.

"There is no fear in love" (1 John 4:18, NAS). I read the words, but peace eluded me. Until I learned all about trust.

That was some time ago, but just the other day I lay on a

hospital bed for an ultra sound. I must have passed my fingers over that lump in my breast ten thousand times before I finally decided to get it checked out. When the doctor pronounced the unexplained lumps of no concern, I realized again that I had been afraid of something nonexistent.

How many things eat us up in worry when the greatest thing we need to avoid is worry itself?

Did you know many people are more afraid of public speaking than of dying? How is it possible to be that possessed with concern over human beings just like us?

My son stands at the top of the stairs, afraid because I turned off the light. How do I let his heart know there is no need for fear, that all is well, that darkness is the same as light when Mama's in the house and he's all tucked in and safe?

And the other night as I wondered how I could handle one more day of settling squabbles, how I would be patient—how could I get my own heart to grasp hold of the grace available to every single mama at the end of her rope?

The greatest gift of Christmas may well be a greater ability to trust. Trust is what breaks through fear to lay hold of, and truly experience in our souls, the presence of Christ.

God chose to reveal the Savior's birth to frightened shepherds.

He came to Joseph, who was afraid and upset.

He came to Mary, a single, vulnerable girl who would trust His heart when He trusted her with the presence of His Son.

When Christ has us, there's nothing in life or death to ruin us.

We begin to walk about with a certain triumph unknown to our fearful hearts, unexplained but for grace—a wild, lavish, free grace breaking through layers of crusted fear on our broken hearts. Grace so extravagant that it permeates straight through the darkness to let the soul know light.

Joseph and Mary embraced the unpredictable events in their engagement, and chose to obey. *They knew the predictability of God, that He was predictably loving, wise, just, and good. Knowing this gave them the ability to trust, and then, obey.*

Resting our confidence in a predictably good, wise, loving Father removes all facets of fear from our lives. Feel your heart begin to tense, then realize it's relaxing, breathing deep, because your soul is aware of a Higher Power. He has this moment of tension just as He has you in your most pleasant places. *You are held.*

My husband is called—sometimes in the dead of night—to head right into the most dangerous situations law enforcement could encounter. He's trained for especially dangerous circumstances and enters houses with crazed men brandishing weapons, refusing to disarm after hours of negotiations.

In the face of true danger, he is less afraid than some of us whose hearts pound over nonexistent danger. He knows his training, his ability, his own shield of safety.

In the same way, we can know our Savior, who says that trust in Him is the weapon which turns *every single dart away.* His banner over us is love. He's prepared a table for us right in the presence of our enemies. Are we feasting, or are we fearing?

"Lord, thank you that there is no fear in your love."

Day 19

"Then the Spirit of the Lord rushed upon him, and although he had nothing in his hand, he tore the lion in pieces as one tears a young goat." Judges 14:6a, ESV

When Manoah and his wife hosted the angel of God and he disappeared into the flame of the sacrifice they offered, they were astounded. Falling on their faces, Manoah thought surely they would die because they had seen the angel of the Lord. But his wife, full of faith, believed God hadn't told them all that only to let them die.

God brought about his word to her, and she gave birth to the son she was promised. She believed, and obeyed the command not to drink wine or take a razor to his head.

She was strong. I love the stories of these women who took God at His word regardless of culture, opinions, or fears. *They took their place in the story of the world because they chose to trust the Creator of the world.*

It's odd that we wouldn't trust Him, when He's the One Who made it all.

Strange that it would enter our minds to doubt the One our very breath is dependent on.

As with everything else, the ruler of this world causes our

minds to wonder whether God really knows what He's doing. Just like he asked Eve in the Garden, "Did God really say
that . . . ?"

Eve knew what God had said, but doubt entered her
mind along with desire for the tantalizing forbidden. When
she reached, took, and ate, her life was forever changed, as
was ours. She didn't see the far-reaching effects of her choices,
didn't know how imperative obedience was when desire wished
to triumph over command.

The things we are tempted with often come cloaked in
goodness and well-being. How many people say, "God wants
me to be happy," then proceed to make a decision that goes
against God's word?

*We're mistaken and deceived when we believe our version
of happiness is of greater value than God's gift of joy.* We trade
the greater for the lesser. We can never know true, lasting joy
apart from the Founder of joy.

Whatever it is that breaks you, makes you want to turn
away from pursuit of Christ to grasp for your own happiness,
remember that when the Spirit of the Lord was on Samson, he
tore the lion in pieces even when he had nothing in his hand.

*He had no weapon to protect himself in the face of dan-
ger. But because the Lord was with him, he had everything he
needed; in fact, what he had was better than his own sword
would have been.*

When you feel as if you have nothing, don't grasp for something apart from the Lord and what He gives you. He gives you
all things good, all things conducive to your highest blessing.
Surrounding vibes of our culture, opinions of others, or your
own fears have little to do with the blessing hidden for you in
walking with the One who made it all.

The true gauge of Christ's presence with you is not the absence of difficulty, but the grace to walk through the trial in victory. Allow the lion to come; allow yourself to be tried. Accept the trial, acknowledge temptation, face your lion. In turn, you will be able to take hold of grace.

We would never need grace if we never had trials. Knowing this enables us not to fear when our own personal lion begins to growl. We are on stage for the display of grace.

When the Spirit of the Lord is on you, you break in pieces the lies and bondage that keep you from joy, blessing, and freedom. Follow hard after Him, and you will find grace pursuing you.

Posture yourself where God is able to overtake you with His grace. When the Spirit comes on you, you will tear in pieces the greatest enemies of your life. Though the lion was strong, Samson was stronger.

He had nothing in his hand, but destroyed the beast that was about to destroy him. So you, when you feel as if you have nothing, know that in Christ, you have everything. When you follow Him, walk with Him, live intimately with Him, then He leads you into fullest joy.

You will defy danger and know no lack.

"Lord, help us to listen well, follow hard,
and not turn aside to other things."

DAY 20

"Come now, let us settle the matter," says the Lord; "Though your sins are like scarlet, they shall be white as snow; though they are red as crimson, they shall be as wool." Isaiah 1:18, NIV

Wind whipped our faces as we sped down the trail on our bikes—I, on the old yard sale bike that always had issues, and my daughter on her used vintage bike.

She was thrilled, and so was I. Leaving the house to face cold, allow our legs to push hard, feel rare winter sunshine splash our faces, and then speed down the hill at breakneck speed all called forth the wild and free in both of us.

Wild and free. Isn't this what we all want to be?

Strange how feeling wind whip about my face makes me want to be free. Strange also how the heart keeps hanging on to things when the Savior came to set us free.

The failures of the past years had been stinging me again. Like a shadow, hounding me with the why, why, why was I so stupid? And why would I think I could have free grace? Of course, my mind knew that grace is unmerited favor, but it's another thing to allow my heart to receive it.

Sometimes I think I can undo my own mistakes and sins if I just feel bad about them one more day. Perhaps another apology, another tear shed, one more time of beating myself up will suffice and bring relief.

But when we beat ourselves up for the rest of our lives, we don't allow God to lift us above the things in our lives.

We bike back up the trail, and push hard. The red berries I see beckon me to stop. They'd look lovely in the house with the white Christmas lights. I pull off a stubborn branch of scarlet red, and I know my sins are just as scarlet. Christ says even though my sins are scarlet, they will be white, as white as the snow we hope to see in the coming days.

Scarlet turned white means it's no longer scarlet. This means that our sins, when washed by the shed blood of Christ, are no longer sins held over us. The shadow we keep feeling is there to condemn us, and Christ says in Romans 8, "There is no condemnation to those who are in Christ Jesus, to those who walk not after the flesh, but after the Spirit."

It's impossible to walk in the Spirit when we keep hanging on to our guilt. Nothing was sufficient to cleanse us save the sacrifice of God's own Son. He came to set us free from the burden of sin, and when we receive His gift, the shadow lifts.

When we don't receive unmerited favor, the shadow stays, clouding our hearts and causing us to walk in even more sin. We can't be free without accepting the gift offered us, and we can't walk in righteousness when we refuse to let go of the shadow darkening our days.

Do we see this, that accepting unmerited favor is the very gateway to the life we long for, that of walking intimately with Christ, that of allowing Him to live His life through us?

Do we see that the Savior came because He knew how scarlet our sins would be, and He didn't want us to have to pay for them?

Do we see that the enemy of our souls tempts us to sin, then turns around and asks us to carry the shame of it for the rest of our days? He knows he has us both ways—once, by committing sin, then later, by carrying the guilt of it.

Freedom never comes by carrying burdens. And accepting God's offer of love is the most loving thing you could do.

If our young child insisted on carrying a heavy bucket of water while we walked by his side wanting to carry it for him, he would stumble, fall, cry, and be unable to enjoy the walk with us. We would mourn his inability to receive the care we want to give; in fact, came to give. He would deprive us of our greatest joy—that of seeing our son blessed, cared for, and happy. In trying to prove his own ability and goodness, he would lose everything we want him to enjoy.

When Christ wants to walk beside us as our friend, removing the load of guilt and turning scarlet into white, we must allow Him, or we will stumble under the load we carry and fall into even more sin. Walking in a cloud of guilt causes us to fall into the ditch we are trying to avoid.

Light never comes from carrying darkness.

Solutions of the kingdom are often counterintuitive. In dying to ourselves, we find true life. In letting go of our own strength, we find the power we've been looking for. In ceasing our own efforts, we accomplish more.

In acknowledging that we have sin, we are freed from it.

I pull hard on the branches of scarlet berries, then lay them all over the house. White lights shine through the red, creating a festive glow. And I know, just as those lights shine brightly, that Christ chases away the darkness in my own heart.

Allow His grace to triumph even over another's sin that could be affecting your life. In the same way you can let go of your own burden, so you can release the burden another brings you.

Refuse to allow him to keep you in darkness by refusing to carry your own or another's darkness.

*"Lord, thank you that you want us to have the freedom
we crave even more than we want it. Thank you for being
a Good Father who delights to give gifts to His children."*

DAY 21

"Whoever can be trusted with very little can also be trusted with much." Luke 16:10a, NIV

The band swelled in magnificent sound across the auditorium, and I sat spellbound. This home school group travels across the country and wins awards in many places. Even small boys work their instruments with ease and accuracy, and the older kids won a competition against college students with their jazz abilities. I was awestruck.

Two of my friends each had four kids on the stage. I knew the amount of hours spent each week driving them to practice, the endless afternoons of faithfulness in small steps toward a greater goal. I knew it wasn't always fun, that at times it seemed mundane and dull.

Concerts were the exception, not the norm. Black dresses, suits and ties, and receptions with friends were the highlight, the aftermath of years of practice. Award-winning trips to our nation's capital were funded by hardworking parents who stuck to the daily grind to provide opportunities like this for their kids.

Sometimes doing small things well leads to big things.

Standing before elaborate structures for photos, winning

admiration of countless judges, causing even critical minds to applaud the beauty of their mixed notes, was possible only because some father was willing to give his afternoon to drive his kids to practice. Some mother dug into her pocketbook even deeper to pay the band teacher. And a great big audience thrilled to the art, the gift, the sound of something magnificently swelling about the room in near-indescribable beauty.

The magnificent is made possible by the mundane. Whether your part is in the magnificent or mundane makes no difference with the Lord, who created each to fill a spot He needed filled in His universe. We need only make sure we don't dream the years away, but actively and faithfully fill our spot.

He gives to each what He wills. Walking closely with Him will lead you right into His heart for you. You need not strive for greatness; only strive to know a great God.

My songwriter friend experienced a depression of sorts following the release of his album. What now? Just the daily routine? A few more years of writing silently, walking faithfully in small things without some exciting goal to work toward? The temptation to dream of the greater while ignoring the small set in, but he knew faithfulness in his daily life is the bedrock for all his greatest ventures.

God looks for a heart enthralled and taken with Himself. The foundation for all things must begin here. If intimacy with God is not the foundation which decides what we do, our accomplishments have a shaky foundation and bring little life to others. Sometimes, this is why people speak truth frequently and have few results, while others, though speaking less, have hearts hungry for the life they offer.

God is Spirit, and He looks for those walking in Spirit and Life.

When the thrill is gone, we return to the steady walk. Each has its place, and each must be embraced if the life is to be full. Never mind if your day doesn't seem great by human expectations—ask God what He thinks of your day.

Walk by His heart more than you live by your own expectations.

The band will continue its practices in the little town on this peninsula in the Pacific Northwest. Mothers will continue to drive their kids, and fathers will dig deep into their wallets for a greater cause. Because of this, a group of kids will travel the world with award-winning music gracing their audience and bringing life to the steady rhythm of time.

The greatest arts are made possible by the greatest faithfulness in the mundane.

"Lord, thank you that we need never feel
fruitless in the small things of life."

Day 22

"Charm is deceitful and beauty is vain, but a woman who fears the Lord is to be praised." Proverbs 31:30, ESV

She dyes her hair blond, even though she's eighty years old. Wearing multiple layers of skin concealer and spending over a hundred dollars a month to disguise her age, she's willing to put up with discomfort for the sake of sporting stiff, high-heeled boots. No one would guess her legs show any sign of age underneath those jeans.

She had always been beautiful, and absorbed the compliments over the years. Praised for her beauty, she believed this was what she had to offer the world. And when age began to make its mark, she felt her worth slipping away.

She'd always thought cosmetic surgery a waste of money, and judged the women who spent thousands on Botox and face-lifts. That is, until her usual faithful creams couldn't defy the steadily increasing number of creases around her eyes.

If beauty had proved her worth to the world, what wouldn't she give to keep it?

She began making calls to the nearest plastic surgeon. Willing her distaste of it all away by reminders of how much younger her appearance would be, she pushed on until the day of surgery arrived.

Something gnawed at the pit of her stomach. Something told her that perhaps she was getting it all wrong. Perhaps she was getting older because that's what happens, and it had nothing to do with her value at all.

She contemplated canceling her appointment and pulled out her Bible. Proverbs chapter 31 opened to her, and she began to read: *"An excellent wife who can find?*

"She is far more precious than jewels.

"The heart of her husband trusts in her, and he will have no lack of gain.

"She does him good, and not harm, all the days of her life.

"She seeks wool and flax, and works willingly with her hands" (v. 10–14).

"She dresses herself with strength and makes her arms strong" (v. 17).

"She opens her mouth with wisdom, and the teaching of kindness is on her tongue" (v. 26).

"Her children rise up and call her blessed; her husband also, and he praises her: 'Many women have done excellently, but you surpass them all.'

"Charm is deceitful and beauty is vain, but a woman who fears the Lord is to be praised.

"Give her of the fruit of her hands, and let her works praise her in the gates" (v. 28–31).

She closed the book with a sigh. The verses seemed to imply that age brought wisdom and valuable experience. What if her husband and family needed and wanted a mother and grandmother more than they wanted her to regain her youthful appearance?

What if the world needed her kindness, love, wisdom, and dil-

igence more than they needed or wanted her beauty? What if even gray hair was a comforting sign of a nurturer, and a grandmotherly appearance benefited the young more than disgusted them?

A deep rest settled her soul as she believed, then embraced her age and calling.

She remembered her younger years, how she'd always noticed and felt drawn to joyful older ladies. She'd always longed for their motherly touch in her life, had loved watching them care for their grown kids and extended family. She'd craved their wisdom, and had asked their advice.

From the day she canceled her surgery, she never looked back. Wrinkles were a sign of love, and gray hair showed the wisdom of years lived. Peace permeated her days where once there was anxiety. Her family loved the change in her demeanor and benefited from the peace in her heart. And not one of them, including her husband, wanted to trade her newfound confidence for a more youthful appearance!

Kara's story resonates in many hearts. Just today, as I walked into a friend's house for lunch, she pointed out some permanent wrinkles that had just emerged on her skin. She laughed about it, and I walked to a mirror to show her my own permanent wrinkles.

We're both healthy moms, now in our thirties. The wrinkles are showing. And there we stood, facing the mirror with the inevitable.

Suddenly, I raised my voice and declared, "We will both embrace our age, including wrinkles when they come!" We high-fived, both of us determined to live the life we admire in other older women. Confidence and joy are attractive, engaging, lovable qualities in mothers and grandmothers, and we determined to mirror them.

Wrinkles will come whether you want them to or not, but confidence and joy are a choice each lady must make personally.

The grandmother at church whom I don't even know personally, draws me in. She's vibrant. She's lovely. She's a nurturer. I approach her one day, and let her know my thoughts on the mother I know she is. She calls me daughter now, and loves the fact that I honor her age, wisdom, and experience. "So many young people," she says, "no longer want to connect with the older generation."

I say grandmothers are needed, loved, highly valued women. We are not used goods when we're older and our beauty fades. We don't need to fight for youth as much as we need to embrace our age. Beauty begins with the heart, and the heart need never grow old.

Let the heart stay young, and all that matters will stay vibrant and fresh.

*"Lord, thank you that our security and worth
do not lie in our fading beauty, but in a much greater,
unchanging love from you."*

DAY 23

"Do not let any unwholesome talk come out of your mouth, but only what is helpful for building others up, according to their needs, that it may benefit those who listen." Ephesians 4:29, NIV

"I have an apprentice," he said, "who can can barely see any good in himself."

The business owner was loving and personable. He could have been greatly frustrated with someone who didn't see his own worth. "I view it as an opportunity," he declared.

His wife chimed in. "When the apprentice says one negative thing about himself, my husband asks him to say five positive things about himself. I'm so proud of him! Lately, everything has been an opportunity to my husband."

I had long been observing this couple, because they had an ability to love and enjoy life like few others I knew. I loved hanging out with them. I loved feeling their love for others. I loved the way they encouraged and loved on their own small kids.

More than anything, I loved the wholesome atmosphere permeating their home, in stark contrast to most places in this world where the very air shouts out need and want of soul.

Our kids ran out the back door to play while the business owner taught my son how to do some forging. Hand to the hammer, my son molded his red-hot piece of iron into a curve while our friend stood holding his infant son.

After a while, our younger son vehemently pushed into the playhouse door and broke it. My heart sank, but our friends smiled and said, "He was feeling strong, and that's what matters right now. Later we may need to talk about carefulness, but for now, let's just allow him to feel his manhood. It's only a door."

I know few parents who would have taken such a positive approach. Most would scold a child, some would even discipline. Few would take a strong look into a child's heart and know the thoughts and feelings there.

Actions are often judged more than the heart, but not here.

A tiny daughter lisps her little wants, and she is heard, listened to, even in the presence of us, their adult guests. Little curly head has all the characteristics of a child well cared for—she's secure, well behaved, and confident in a quiet way. Mommy and Daddy require obedience, but they also listen in, tune in, gaze carefully, and love hard.

These people are encouragers, they are listeners, and they love well. As the business owner drives along with his apprentice, some life stories tumble out that the rest of us will never hear about. What is said in the truck stays in the truck. But that apprentice is learning a whole lot more than a business; he's learning about *wholeness of heart and peace of soul.* The business owner is giving, again, in more than tangible ways.

Some of the best giving comes in unseen, but heartfelt, ways such as encouragement and listening in when you could move on or ignore. Choosing to give when there is no obligation to do so shows a heart connected to God, Who is always giving in redemptive ways.

This couple is a gift to all who know them, not because they always please everyone, but because they don't. My friend is great about saying "no" when she cannot peacefully do something. But in declining, she shows love, and in the end, people know her for radiance and encouragement.

I was there when she won an award on our team for being "Miss Sunshine." And I'll always be grateful for the boost in my own life from hanging out with two friends *who view life as an opportunity*, who focus so much on the good that the bad fades into the distance.

Did you know you can choose to love so hard that discord takes the last seat rather than the first?

That you can choose gratefulness for so many things that you don't even want to utter discontentment any longer? *That when you choose to rejoice in the rainbow rather than complain about the rain, the sun shines in your soul and you are loath to give way to shadows?*

There's glory, friends. There's joy. When you choose to encourage all those around you, your life will also change.

Leave the critics inhaling their own dust. As for you, be a splash of sunshine on someone's path today!

"Lord, help us to give light to another's day today. Help us not to cast shadows, but to give love forward, lavishly."

Day 24

"Whoever finds his life will lose it, and whoever loses his life for my sake will find it." Matthew 10:29, ESV

The sun dipped low over the horizon of snow-blown fields where long rows of cattle lined feeding troughs, chowing down in the dark coldness. I wanted to leave the car and run through the frozen sagebrush, sit in the snow, tune into all things wild and earthy, and listen for the sound of howling coyotes.

Their sound sweeps me with simultaneous dread and delight. I've a love-drenched heart for these fields, where once we lived in an old farmhouse desperately in need of paint and a new roof. There, a moose ambled across the lawn one day before he disappeared over the hill of yet one more fertile wheat field. There, coyotes howled at night and owls whooed in the trees outside our bedroom window.

And there, our son learned to love country. His heart has never sunk into marine life as it has into earth, fields, and farm. Living on the water's edge hasn't called his soul out as those ageless rolling hills once did.

It takes something special to call our souls, something beyond ourselves, something vast and wonderful. Sometimes, what we look for within ourselves is only found apart from ourselves.

If we save our own puny lives, we end up with nothing but our lonely desolate selves.

If we break into sacrificial love, we gain dividends of love in return. The rich in heart were never brought to satiation of soul by hanging on to their own small lives in self-protection.

When our hearts contain only ourselves, we end up with just that, a brittle, shallow, small heart with only enough room for our own narrow thoughts. *Our hearts desire to be called into something greater than ourselves.*

The essence of this greatness is love, is God.

Break into given love, dare lay yourself down for another, and you will find your walls enlarged, your gates opened, your heart made rich with the presence of many beautiful souls. Weave your life into others so your single strand of thread has a myriad of color braided into it, thus creating something more than your one lonely life.

Your single strand will have to weave, bend, and give to allow other strands to wrap themselves around it. It will feel smothered at times, will feel lost as it's wrapped round and round again. *But in the end, it's blended into a beautiful tapestry of color made possible only by given love.*

We drive ahead of the blazing sunset, and I keep turning my head to stare at its vibrant color. Just on Sunday, my friend and I had stood at the well-lit tree in the church sanctuary and held our stomachs as we imagined our own little ones cold and hungry like the refugee mothers' kids we were concerned about.

Embrace the pain of another, and you end up holding more love than if you'd hung on to yourself for the love of your own life.

Dare take up those papers for foster care.

Dare travel to a refugee camp to dish up soup.

Dare write that large amount on your check rather than the smaller one.

Dare tell your kids that the floor under the tree will be less loaded with gifts so that one more child will have a warm blanket to sleep with.

Dare do away with the talk and walk the walk. Because when you do away with your own life, you end up truly finding life. When you refuse to hang your one strand of thread alone, you reach out and pull more strands into your own life—and you end up with more heart.

Hearts meshed together in all their need and brokenness create a circle, a union of sorts. *We were made to live together.* Dare unveil your broken places to one another because you dare believe that nothing is meant to stay broken, and in Christ all things are whole. Including you. Including them.

Hold out your heart, then hold out your hand. Give an extra squeeze next time you're in the crowd. Write that note when the thought comes to mind. Pull that pair of cozy socks off the shelf and hand them to another in a simple brown bag.

When walls are up, don't be afraid. It's OK not to penetrate someone's mask; it's not OK to pass them by.

Living given love means we view all people as valuable, and difficult places only call for more soul gazing. Perhaps the walls are up because no one has ever seen clear through to the heart. Perhaps they've never felt given love. Perhaps they don't even know why they live like they do. Perhaps God wants to give you wisdom on how to reach the deepest places that began formation long before they were even aware.

Blindness is a soul unaware of freedom, of love. If you see clearly, grab the hand and guide them to light.

Love encapsulates our posture before the cross, and seals our business with Christ.

The lady waiting in the emergency room for her aging mother looks weary, tired. I whisper it to her, "You are doing an amazing thing. I admire you."

She's living given love, despite the difficulty. Her soul is rich, her heart paved with thoughts of Christ. In all of it, her life will become the better for living given. *Stretch out your hand to others, and in some odd way you will find your hands filled in the very act of giving it all away.*

Wrap another's need and brokenness around your own heart, and you will find the thread of your life not to be alone and spent, but rich and beautiful. Woven all around and through your single strand will be many other strands—and together, they will create a beautiful weave all through your life.

"Father, thank you that living given love only causes our hearts to be more full of it."

DAY 25

"Come to me, all you who are weary and burdened, and I will give you rest. Take my yoke upon you and learn from Me, for I am gentle and lowly in heart, and you will find rest for your souls. For my yoke is easy and my burden is light." Matthew 11:28–30, NIV

Many of us run from our brokenness rather than embrace it.

We don't want to be broken, poor, or at a loss. We want to be whole.

Some of us turn to things, others turn to people. Still another may turn to accomplishment or ministry or a myriad of other things to ease the ache.

The fix works for a moment.

The thrill of accomplishment lasts a while, until you need the next one. Then you may look around and start comparing yourself to others. You see the pretty girl with the smile on her face and decide that she is happy, "of course," because in her shoes, who wouldn't be? On the other hand, there's that friend whose trials seem endless, who never catches a break, who can't seem to keep her head above the water that never stops pouring into her life. Both are trying to find what was lost in the Garden—complete wholeness of body, soul, and spirit.

Here, two pathways meet: the person of whom it's said, "Of course she's happy," and the person of whom it is said, "How could she possibly be happy?"

At some point in the journey, we all collide into the same quest for meaning. No one can find what she truly needs in another person, place, or thing. *The man, woman, or child whose life brims over with blessing may know the same quest for satisfaction as the person who has nothing.*

That empty spot is there to lead us to Christ. Those empty-handed ones who find it are more blessed of soul than those who enjoy external or human gifts but don't know union with Christ.

The girl who grasps for blessing beyond her reach feels as if she'd be all set for a lifetime of joy if she could only attain. But the girl who already knows the blessing realizes the same quest for more. Here, hearts converge, and here, they all relate to each other.

Seeking for meaning must lead us to the Source of our existence, Jesus Christ, "for Whom all things were created, whether they be in heaven or earth" (Colossians 1:16).

The hungry of heart will always be hungry unless they learn to know and experience the presence of Christ.

We may look to other things to satisfy, to bring meaning, to give us the thrill. But nothing suffices to fill the void save the presence of Christ. He may lead us to other wonderful things, but they are never meant to replace Him. He may gift us, but these things are never meant to replace the gift of Himself. He may even allow us to feel dissatisfaction when we don't pursue the things we're gifted in, but *our own gifts are here to make known the glories of Himself, the ultimate gift.*

Enjoy your life, but enjoy Him more.

Seek to use your gifts, but know that your ultimate purpose is to magnify the Ultimate Gift. *Barrenness of soul comes when we live as though we are the end of all things, rather than knowing the end purpose of our lives is to bring glory to the Creator of it all.*

We were never meant to be the story; we were created to play a part in His story. *Our own happiness isn't the story.* Christ is glorified when we allow Him to fill the spots no one else will ever fill.

Take heart, soul whose life has been missing the joys and blessing known to many. *You are on a swifter road to finding the Ultimate Gift than many who've been blessed with many gifts.*

Your brokenness is the surest road to wholeness, because we all need wholeness and the broken see it first. Christ came to be the Physician, but the whole do not always see their need for one. Those who don't see their need never experience the healing.

When life is rocky, you get to be carried, and being carried is what all of us need. There's no better place to be than in the arms of Christ. As He carries you, He will also lead you. As He leads you, you will know blessing. As you are blessed, you will give Him all credit, and thus, His purpose for you will be fulfilled.

Idolatry is anything you hang on to for your happiness more than Christ. Anything you think you absolutely cannot live without for satisfaction, significance, or affection and love. Christ is more than His creation, and He wants to be most to your heart.

Human lack may always be felt in one sense or another, because we are human. *There is no condemnation in feeling lack—there is only loss when we don't allow Christ to take His place as greater than any lack we may know.* His fullness always surpasses emptiness. And it is here that He wants your soul to abide. Hanging on to earthly or human things in place of Christ will lead you downward no matter how much (or how little) you have.

When you are honest with the Lord about your lack, He will show Himself most real to you. When you admit your chaos of heart, He will show you His peace. When you cry your hottest tears with your face lifted to the sky in a silent plea, He sweeps you with stillness. *Never be afraid of owning your grief, because in doing so you own His grace.*

The stronger your lack, the greater His manifested peace becomes in your life.

"His yoke is easy and His burden is light."

Do you add Christianity to your life, or is Christ your life?

Life is more about the glory of Christ than it is about our own happiness. But when we know the glories of Christ, we find satisfaction of heart, peace of soul, and truest joy. The gifts we may wish would grace our lives are not to be compared with the Ultimate Gift.

We can never out-give the Ultimate Giver.

"Father, thank you that we all converge into the same quest for meaning; that our humanness doesn't end with one, but includes us all; that in the end, we all need the same grace."

Day 26

"Therefore, having received this ministry by the mercy of God, we do not lose heart." 2 Corinthians 4:1, ESV

"For God who said, 'Let light shine out of darkness,' has shone in our hearts to give the light of the knowledge of the glory of God in the face of Jesus Christ." 2 Corinthians 4:6, ESV

I joined my husband in the living room and picked up my laptop. But my fingers remained nearly immobile and I found it impossible to write.

All day I'd been hounded with insecurities, fears, and self-hatred, and a gnawing sense of depression hung over me just like the clouds had been hanging over our county for the past few months.

It was my husband's birthday. I hated myself for being so low on his special day. Thank goodness we had celebrated with a party the night before or I'd have felt like a complete failure.

I gave up writing, picked up my Bible, and found a solitary spot in the backyard. Honesty with the Lord has become my new default since I've learned I don't need to perform for Him. He picks me up when I let it all out and hold nothing back.

I opened my Bible to a random spot and the first verse I read mentioned hope. *"Since we have such hope, we are very bold"* (2 Corinthians 3: 12a).

I read on: *"Where the Spirit of the Lord is, there is freedom"* (v. 17b).

And then, "And we all, with unveiled face, beholding the glory of the Lord, are being transformed into the same image from one degree of glory to another" (v. 18a).

It didn't end there. My eyes skimmed to the next chapter, and I found this: *"Therefore, having this ministry by the mercy of God, we do not lose heart"* (4:1).

Paul goes on to say we've put aside the works of our flesh, because "God, who said, 'Let light shine out of darkness,' has shone in our hearts to give the light of the knowledge of the glory of God in the face of Jesus Christ" (4:6).

Immediate peace flooded my heart. Here was God Himself, through Paul's writing, telling me there's hope. I knew there was no accident in me landing on those verses. I picked up my Bible and walked inside with a certain spring to my step.

A few hours later my sister called me and out of the blue gave me the sweetest words of encouragement. Days later, my brother-in-law said, "You're doing an awesome job as mama and wife—Bravo!!"

And a few days later, I received a text from a friend that addressed the very thing I was down about. Then, another text from a friend who said she had a dream, and in the dream I was discouraged, asking for prayer. The verse the Lord gave her in the dream for me blew me away—it was exactly what I needed to hear in that very particular situation.

I was amazed. Not one, but multiple things in succession.

God cares this much for me? To meet me in a dark hour with one thing right after another, so specific and personal?

God is personal, highly in tune with the deepest workings of your heart, because He made your heart.

Friends, it's OK if you haven't found all the answers to your need or circumstance. Let it all out to the Lord and allow Him to breathe hope into you. He's the God of hope and He causes light to shine out of darkness.

That night I tucked the kids in bed and tidied up the house. My husband was working nights, so the house was empty and still as I picked up my phone. A link caught my eye, and I opened it to read more about hope.

If we're waiting around for someone else to change our lives, we have it wrong and it may never happen, the writer declared. If your life needs change, reach out to make it happen. No one owes us. If we live as though they do, we may always be missing out on many things.

If we need help, we need to reach out for it.

If you enjoy painting, you're the one to pick up the brush or it will never happen.

You may not have things handed to you, but you can reach out for them. Be brave.

Take risks.

Ask God for what you need.

Know that everything good warrants sacrifice and risk.

Nothing can destroy you unless you allow it. **Nothing.**

Allow God to unlock your heart and set you free. Pursue Him and all the good things He's gifted you with. Live fully!

"Lord, thank you that we don't need to hang about the low zone any longer. Thank you that we get to soar."

DAY 27

"So you shall speak to all who are gifted artisans, whom I have filled with the spirit of wisdom . . ." Exodus 28:3, NKJV

He was a pediatric anesthesiologist.
She was a plastic surgeon.

This girl was a volunteer.

That guy a registered nurse.

One person brought us water.

Another showed us a quiet room to catch a few winks of sleep.

She was a surgeon who would return in just a few hours after a bit of sleep.

She was a nurse with all the marks of sympathy showing on her face to bring us comfort.

Those few days with my son in pain brought us healing delivered in so many various ways by so many various people doing many varied things. The nurse who brought us water was important, as was the surgeon.

I pondered this. Purpose. What is it, and how do we find and fulfill it?

God fills people with the gifts He wants them to have, then calls them forth at the time needed. This is why it is so counterproductive to try to be someone else, or not be content with your own place in life.

Freedom comes in knowing God created you with a purpose. He painted you, so when you complain about yourself, you are complaining against the Author of Beauty Himself. He knew what He wanted! Dissatisfaction in who you are is allowing your mind to be shaped by things lesser than God.

Take the plunge and choose to believe that you are purpose-filled in His sight. Life and beauty will open their arms to you, and you will dare to dream again, this time in freedom.

It doesn't matter whether or not you are the best at what you do: simply give the world your best and you will bring good to those around you.

God never asked you to be the best—He asks you to give your all.

Have you ever noticed how often the Lord uses commonly placed people for some of His grandest missions?

"Then Amos answered and said to Amaziah, 'I was no prophet, nor the son of a prophet, but *I was a* sheep-breeder *and a tender of sycamore fruit.* But the Lord took me as I followed the flock, and the Lord said to me, "Go, prophesy to my people Israel"'" Amos 7:14–15, NKJV.

In pondering life, its meaning, and what our purpose is, it is easy to want the glorious, glamorous, and seemingly more important things. But again and again in scripture we see Jesus appearing to shepherds, anointing a shepherd boy to be king, choosing Mary from a small town to be the mother of His son, asking fishermen to follow Him, living in a small town Himself, even being born in a stable.

Greatness as we perceive it is not as God sees it, and purpose in life does not come from pursuing greatness, but pursuing a purposeful God.

"For the eyes of the Lord run to and fro throughout the face of the whole earth, to show Himself strong on behalf of those whose heart is loyal to Him" 2 Chronicles 16:9a, NKJV.

Whether you are a mother, a teacher, a babysitter, a nurse, or a doctor, when life is lived for the Lord, no one is more purpose filled than the other because Jesus is our purpose, and He gives each of us a task.

Focus on Him, and He will lead you to fulfill your mission.

Jesus Himself was born in a stable, laid in a manger, raised in a small town by a mother whose reputation had long been ruined. He was a carpenter until age thirty. This was Lord of Lords and King of the Universe! Still, He fulfilled his destiny.

I wonder why we, as mere human beings, are less content to play our part on this earth than He was.

With such an example, I daresay we are struck with a vision that will hopefully blind us to all discontentment and jealousy.

"Lord, thank you that knowing you sets us free to fill our purpose with delight and satisfaction."

DAY 28

"For You formed my inward parts; You covered me in my mother's womb.

"I praise You, for I am fearfully and wonderfully made; Marvelous are Your works, my soul knows it very well.

"My frame was not hidden from You, when I was being made in secret, skillfully wrought in the lowest parts of the earth.

"Your eyes saw my substance, being yet unformed. And in Your book they were all written, the days fashioned for me, when as yet there were none of them.

"How precious also are Your thoughts to me, Oh God! How great is the sum of them!

"If I should count them, they they would be more in number than the sand;

"When I awake, I am still with You." Psalm 139:13–18, NKJV

When God created you, He gave you unique and special qualities.

You are unable to give glory unless you receive God's glory, unless you see you are destined for greatness (whatever that may look like), unless you know you are a piece of God's passion which He created without answering to another for His creativity. He certainly doesn't answer to us, His creations!

He is the ultimate artist and has plans for His painting.

Ever seen the look on a child's face when you ask him what he wants to do when he grows up? Unabashed delight as he shares great and awesome plans. He knows he can do it!

It takes only about fifteen years for a child's spirit to wilt and have him believe all he can do is small things. Why? Why are we not full of passion, and give that passion to children so that, at age fifteen, they still believe they were destined for great things?

You only fly as high as you aim your sights. And you won't aim your sights high if you despise yourself.

God is your artist! Pursue your calling, whether it fits your own perception of greatness or not. If God called you to it, it is great.

A dear sister wrote out these purposes of her heart:

"I purpose to channel my energies into *speaking life* to the spiritually and emotionally dead.

I purpose to overcome evil by *binding up the broken hearted* and pointing them to beauty.

I purpose to *fight for justice* by being an advocate for the misused.

I purpose to *be a voice* against the victimization of the vulnerable.

I purpose to *fight for the freedom of souls* in spiritual and emotional captivity.

I purpose to *live out sacrificial love* without expectations of my own.

I purpose to *stay connected* to the eternal purpose of ministering joy to the mourning.

I purpose to *shine Christ's hope* to hearts overtaken with despair.

I purpose to *keep my eyes, ears, and heart sensitized* to signs of hidden pain.

I purpose to *know the heart of God* and allow my heart to be broken with His.

I purpose to *seek justice, love mercy, and walk humbly."*

This dear lady was born into a large family of twelve. Her passion for others began at a young age, and everywhere she went, she sought out the lonely, hurting, or sad. In large crowds she was drawn to the most vulnerable.

She presently finds herself in Greece surrounded by refugees, and even there, is serving tea to the most vulnerable of all — trafficked women who have fled the Middle East and are now stranded on the island with nowhere to go. She sits with them, listens to their stories, serves them tea . . . and then she fights for them until an agency agrees to take them to a safe place. They kiss her face, they weep, and when she is in need, they care for her in return.

But it didn't start in Greece. She lived like that, just like that, at home in her parents' house, on a regular Sunday in a small church, and in her job at a local grocery in a small town.

So can you. Purpose to live like Jesus lived, to reach out always, everyday, and your life will change. He says we are His hands and feet. If your life is empty and apathetic, remind yourself that a disciple of Jesus has the deepest passion to live for, because He calls us to live like He lived and to walk with the hurting just like He did.

When we do, life opens up because our souls come alive when we breathe the same breath He breathes.

Our souls were made to dance to the eternal. Nothing short of that will satisfy.

Matthew 25:14–30 speaks of a man who went on a journey and gave talents (coins in biblical times) to three of his servants. Both men with five and two talents busily traded their money and made more. The man with one talent found a place to hide it and just left it there until his master returned. When the master returned, he praised the servants who used and cultivated what they were given. The lazy servant was reprimanded and cast out.

This parable is the source of our English word "talents," meaning skills or abilities. We may personally feel like the servant who was given one talent, and feel intimidated by others who have more. Because of insecurities, we hide and do not cultivate what we do have. We fret over what others may think of us instead of shining where we are called to be.

We are a bit like a mountain flower refusing to bloom because it is not a fertilized rose in some oft-viewed neighborhood yard. How ridiculous, we say! We love finding flowers in obscure places, and they mean more to us when they bloom in less desirable locations.

Every person has something to offer. When we offer what we do have, we grow more, and we honor the Lord by walking in what He designed.

The Lord needs us to bloom regardless of where we are planted. Whether you are a fisherman's wife in a lonely hut in Alaska, or a pastor's wife living the fishbowl life in some mega church in San Diego, each of you has a responsibility to find what you are gifted in, and to function in those gifts.

"God, who at various times and in various ways spoke in time past to the fathers by the prophets" Hebrews 1:1.

See how God wants to speak in various times and in various ways?

When you notice a deep desire within to do something, pay attention. It may be the very thing you were born to do. If you love painting, by all means buy a brush and set to creating art! If you thrive in needy situations, take note and realize God is calling you to reach out to hurting people. If you love visiting the sick, learn all you can about how to minister to them the best way. Simply function in what you do best and you will be purpose-filled.

Having purpose brings joy and intimacy with the Lord, and is one of the best counters for depression.

"Father, help us to dance to the eternal more than we dance to any other person or thing."

Day 29

"We have been with child, we have been in pain; We have, as it were, brought forth wind; We have not accomplished any deliverance in the earth . . ." Isaiah 26:18, NKJV

Ah! I've felt like that so many times—worn out physically with my heart dull, but I've also felt exuberant joy after labor and known I've labored in the Lord. Some of those joys came when I shut out the world and took time for things that mattered, things that can be pushed aside easily in the course of a busy life. Deliberately backing away from life to take time for that specific thing on your heart can make all the difference.

For me, it is writing. For you, it may be something else. Perhaps reading or business, running or leading study groups. Whatever it is, find what makes your heart "run on full," and do it with joy.

Often, the things that bring us the most joy are the very things we are meant to do.

So, when we are frustrated, tired, and lifeless, let's pause a moment and ask God if we are giving energy to the things He designed us to do. Let's not "give birth to wind!"

God's heart is for you to see your value and know that nothing and no one can keep you from bringing beauty and life into the world. In fact, His life in you will shine even more when all around you is dark. So take courage, women in hard places!

You were not meant to go down in the storm—you were meant to ride the waves.

Do your very best for the Lord instead of for people. When we build for ourselves, we labor in vain (as did the people who built the Tower of Babel in Genesis 11:4–9); when we build for the Lord, we see His greatness far surpassing any person or situation and are able to stand strong and keep building.

We were born to create because once we, too, were created. But we were born to create for the Lord. Having this in mind will keep us strong whether or not others around us are building for the Lord.

Often times, we wait to build until our circumstances change. God's desire is for us to build right where we are. Look at the words He gave His people when they were in the land of their captivity:

"Thus says the Lord of hosts, the God of Israel, to all who were carried away captive, whom I have caused to be carried away from Jerusalem to Babylon: Build houses and dwell in them; plant gardens and eat their fruit. Take wives and beget sons and daughters; and take wives for your sons and give your daughters to husbands, so that they may bear sons and daughters—that you may be increased there, and not diminished.

"And seek the peace of the city where I have caused you to be carried away, and pray to the Lord for it; for in its peace you will have peace" (Jeremiah 29:4–7, NKJV).

When circumstances become difficult, do not retreat. Embrace the situation; lean into it.

If those around you are not what they should be, there is even more reason for you to build with purpose.

God is in the business of building, creating, working. Let's work with Him and for Him!

"Lord, help us to build, design, and create those things
you've gifted us in regardless of where we are.
Help us know that you speak over our lives more than
circumstances speak into our lives."

Day 30

"You are the salt of the earth, but if the salt has lost its taste, how shall its saltiness be restored? It is no longer good for anything, but to be thrown out and trampled under people's feet. You are the light of the world; a city set on a hill cannot be hidden. Nor do people light a lamp and put it under a basket, but on a stand, and it gives light to all in the house.

"In the same way, let your light shine before others, so that they may see your good works and give glory to your Father Who is in heaven." Matthew 5:13–16, ESV

I pressed my forehead against the plane window as the evening sun blazed across the heavens.

Lifted into the glorious, so far above the earth below, makes me want to throw myself all over again into something and Someone so much greater.

The largeness of Christ amazes me. How He takes me and all that concerns me into His hands time and time and time again.

But I cannot believe how small my own brain is, my thoughts excluding the Great and Good for the pitiful and narrow. I look around at people instead of God. My smallness makes me think that largeness consists of people and how they affect me, when it is God and how His love changes me.

On all fronts we thirst for approval, affirmation, and love. We want to do, believe, live in such a way as to gain intimacy with those who touch our lives. We look around instead of *up*. And when we do so, God and His ways become vague to us, perhaps even dubious.

It's as if we truly are daughters of Eve and need to reckon with the fact. The fact that when humanity fell into sin, it would take a miracle, a rebirth, to make us aware of what is really true.

For the truth to burn, even sear into our very souls that life is not as it appears. The tangible must give way to the spiritual. The world around us is passing, people are a shadow, and culture changes. That earth and our humanness will pass away, and people live for such an incredibly short time.

We really are a breath. A puff across the expanse of a greater picture.

Why in all the world are we so taken with the earth?

It's easy to say as I glide through the heavens and stare at the vast, endless blue yonder with the sun blazing orange across the sky.

But what about tomorrow as we all wake for another day? What about that random person who needs love to wear shoes, to have hands and feet? What about that child who will be drawn to our faith, not by our frustrated efforts to live righteously, but by seeing the effect Jesus has on our lives when we replace our love for the passing with His heart?

God is real. There is a reason we drive our cars, go to work, eat our food, have good times, and all the while we know we were created for something greater.

It's because we really were.

And I don't know about you, but I would much rather

stake my life on something that always was, presently is, and always will be. Allow the Infinite to permeate the finite, allow the Creator to determine the created, and know mortality is but for a season before immortal life is offered us.

"Lord, thank you that we get to stake our lives on something eternal, and let your light shine through us."

Day 31

"In Him we have obtained an inheritance, having been predestined according to the purpose of Him Who fills all in all." Ephesians 1:11, ESV

God created us with an unquenchable longing for the Infinite, giving us a thirsty desire that will not be quenched by anything less than God Himself. We were born to be part of something greater than ourselves.

This is why people want to be a part of sports (or watching them), try to create an online persona, or are thrilled with the hero in a movie even when most people are not heroes. At the end of the day, we are all dissatisfied with life unless it's wrapped up in something greater than we are.

In a postmodern world, the ageless cathedrals and christened elegance of the Middle Ages are less common, while many people try to find meaning in smaller stories of their own making, in progress and modernism, or in the social media world.

We were born into a finite sphere within a vast, infinite plan. Our hearts are made to dance to the eternal.

Perhaps this is why we feel frustrated when we try to control our lives; when we try to satisfy our longings with things; when we cease to realize that *the greatest wonder we will ever know is eternal, and we are but a small part of a plan birthed in an infinite realm.*

Friends, at the end of the day, our souls were made to dance to the eternal more than they were ever meant to enjoy any other person, thing, or activity. The emptiness inside is a mere indication that there is a void to be filled with something more than you (or anyone else) can offer.

When you stand face-to-face with reality as it is and not as it appears, you start to see a picture that extends beyond yourself. You see that you are formed as part of a larger plan that has existed from the beginning, and which we get to have part in. It is vast enough to excite deepest wonder, and exciting enough to engage the most adventurous thrill seeker.

Sometimes what we really need is to give up what our flesh wants for what our entire being truly needs. Perhaps this is why some of the happiest people I know are those who are most excited about God, and most engaged in His work.

"Lord, help us to be convinced that meaning will never come from within ourselves, but only from you."

Day 32

"For you were bought with a price; so glorify God in your body." 1
Corinthians 6:20, ESV

Some of us have a difficult time realizing we are an asset to
this world, not a liability.

For many of us, we're most comfortable offering service
to others because it makes us feel like an asset instead of a liability. The most difficult thing is for us to accept service from
others because we feel like we are putting others out, like we
are taking, like somehow we will end up wearing out another.

Each one of us is an asset in this world. Every asset needs
certain things in place to continue being of use. Nothing of
material matter can do well if its environment is unsuited to
its particular need. So you, even though you are an asset, need
certain things from others.

To receive those things rather than try to pretend you don't
need them is to further your purpose and make you more fruitful. You are an asset in this world because a good creator God
breathed purpose for you and in you when He planned your
very makeup. Your physical and emotional makeup is not a
mistake. The vulnerable areas of your life where you find yourself most in need are also not mistakes.

When you see this, you are able to receive. When you receive, you prosper and become more whole. *When you quit beating yourself up for having needs, you are more able to find solutions to your needs.*

Being "needless" does not prove you to be an asset. A tree dies without water; this does not imply that a tree is not a useful part of the world. If a tree were to stand tall, denying its need for water, it would die and no longer be useful. Trees are one of the most valuable things in our world, yet they, too, need certain conditions to survive.

Doing too many hard things to prove yourself can turn you into a hard person. You were created a human being before you were a human doer.

Today, reach out and don't be afraid to ask. You are, after all, an asset just like those around you!

Setting yourself on a blazing fire to keep others warm ensures that you will burn out and they have less warmth than before. God wants to bless your heart, not just your service.

When you view yourself as a liability rather than an asset, you render yourself useless, and in turn, you become bored. You simply don't see the purpose and value God places on your life.

A Christian is only bored when she's not pursuing the purpose God created her for.

"Ludwig Van Beethoven wrote, 'Tones sound, and storm, and roar about me until I have set them down in notes." Many of us don't have notes pouring into our heads, but we have stirrings of the heart calling us to the things we want to do, and are good at doing, because God wants us to do them. Our voice comes both directly and indirectly, in word and in action to the world around us.

"None of us will ever accomplish anything excellent or commanding except when he listens to this whisper which is heard by him alone."—Ralph Waldo Emerson

"Father, thank you that in your world, all of us get to be an asset. Thank you that we all get to receive as well as give."

Day 33

"The Lord your God is in your midst, a mighty one who will save; he will rejoice over you with gladness; he will quiet you by his love; he will exult over you with loud singing." Zephaniah 3:17, ESV

The water's clear, silent, and still today, and birds soar over it side by side. I'm listening in on a still, calm, quiet Voice letting me know I'm OK. I'm more than OK; I'm held, loved, and accepted. I'm *created*.

Get this—I'm *created*. This means deliberately fashioned and shaped and formed because God wanted me a certain way.

If I'm created by God, why would I base my worth on the opinions of another one of His fallible creations? Why not rather seek identity in my Creator alone? Isn't He infallible, perfect? And hasn't He said that He formed me in the womb, exactly how He wanted me?

He never said I was good enough; in fact, He says we are not good enough, but He's come to grace us with His good love. He washes us clean and does a heart makeover, changing us and revamping our lives. *When we cease trying to feel good about ourselves, we are finally able to accept God's goodness and perfection.*

True security will never come from positive thinking. You cannot pound in your head enough that you are worthy, good, and awesome. True security comes from seeing that we are in need of redemption each and every day, as is everyone around us—and Christ came to gift us with a whole new set of values and truths that are much greater than our own or anyone else's.

The things people say or don't say matter little in light of what God says. Because they are also in need of redeeming thoughts, and sometimes they're not seeing clearly—which is the only reason hurts exist to begin with.

What your fellow human beings think of you is of little worth compared to God's thoughts of you. And truth is, He's so full of mercy that He invites you rather than rejects you.

He forgives you rather than condemns you.

He sees your human pain as His opportunity to show you His supernatural healing.

He loves you so extravagantly that you cannot help but shed the nasty in exchange for His lovely.

You don't stay in your muck when you stay in His grace.

Do we see this, that patting ourselves on the back with our own positive thinking is counterproductive, because we will never, ever be good enough without owning our depravity and receiving free, boundless grace that changes us from the inside out?

You will never feel good about those gaping needs in your life. Trying to feel good about *yourself* means you're not owning your needs and allowing God's own goodness to overtake you, changing those needs.

Because free grace brings with it free Lordship. In the wrapped gift of free grace, comes the wrapped gift of Ultimate Lordship.

There's a great difference between positive thinking and positive faith. One brings more turmoil; the other, endless peace. One tells you you're good when you're not; the other fills you with goodness not your own while it cleanses you from needs all your own.

One lulls you to sleep when you need to wake up; the other lifts you out of your own muck and *changes you.*

Positive thinking never implies repentance of any kind, whereas positive faith can only settle in the heart right along with a turning away from all you are, to all Christ is.

True faith works from the inside out, because positive faith, not positive thinking, removes our yuck, clears our minds, settles our emotions, changes our relationships, and makes us new. You cannot have an encounter with God without encountering change. *We cannot claim true saving grace without allowing that grace to truly save us.* Thinking positive thoughts about yourself is of much lesser importance than allowing positive faith to turn your life around.

Christ never asked us to feel good about ourselves. He does ask us to own our need of Him, and give our own low lives in exchange for the good one He has in store for us.

Positive faith is the only way of revamping our thoughts into lasting security.

Today, dare feel good about God. He will then show you His love, which will turn you into a person of goodness, peace, and rest with God, yourself, and all those around you—regardless of where they fall on the scale of giving you what you need, or not.

Because true peace never came from within you or from anyone else; true peace comes from hosting Christ and owning His words to you *in spite of yourself, and in spite of those around you.*

Today, I declare my freedom to believe God's heart toward me, and for me.

Today, I dare move past and beyond.

Today, I dare soar above still waters, just like the birds outside my living room window.

In resting, I bring new dimensions of life to all those around me, because being still in God's presence always brings more beauty than trying to be good enough.

"Lord, thank you for the amazing peace and vibrancy that overtakes us when we cease looking to ourselves or others for life, and look to you instead for each word you speak over us."

Day 34

"*Though He slay me, I will hope in Him.*" *Job 13:15a, ESV*

I took his hand, this small child of mine, and led him to the fence. The wire thistles stood tall and cow pies hid in the weeds. Who knows, perhaps even snakes slithered in the grass.

But there were blackberries just beyond. I encouraged him to follow, and he did. Standing before tall thistles, he bravely lifted one leg after another and navigated his way through, where I stood in pride over his effort and bravery.

We made it through, his hand holding tightly to mine, and there they were, those luscious, gigantic, purple berries we savor each summer.

But then, we had to return the same way we came. This time he was tired, and as we neared the thistle patch, I stooped and picked him up. He wrapped his little arms round my neck and clung tightly as we both conquered those evil little prickles.

I set him down on the other side. He stooped low over a flower and chattered with delight, already oblivious to what we had just navigated.

I stood there, pondering. I love him, love him with a depth I can't even describe. Is this how Jesus feels about me?

I have to believe it is, but even more. I'm honored He uses

a mother's love to describe His own, but somehow it seems too much, still, that He should love me with such passion. That I should be able to trust Him even more than my own son trusts me. That He knows how much I can take, when I need to walk right through these thistles in my life, or be carried right above them where they can't even grab at my heels.

He knows how to take me to the other side. My son trusted when I asked him to walk through, and he trusted when I carried him. He knows Mama. He knows my love. Daily, we smile and laugh and hug and talk. *He knows me.* And as thistles threatened to prick his legs, he trusted in that truth, that knowledge.

And when we know God, when we are held by Him and life turns into relationship more than religion, this is when we absolutely know we can trust. We talk with Him, we host His Spirit, we are loath to part with His presence because we've found Him to satiate us to the core of who we are. Truth permeates, truth reigns.

It's all in the knowing. We trust because we know He is good, like Job did when his children died, his belongings were stolen, and he fell sick with boils. Even his wife asked him to curse God and die.

But Job? Never! He knew, like I know many years later, that God is good, that He is not to be compared to circumstances or people in a fallen world, that He reigns far and high above.

But Job didn't know he was on trial before the God of the Universe and the powers of darkness. *He really didn't know, friends.* In reading his story, we know all about it and sigh with relief that Job dared trust. But we read the aftermath, the grand culmination of Satan's defeat when Job dared say, "Though He slay me, I will hope in Him."

Satan had tried every way to get him to say the opposite. I'm fascinated that God is willing to take risks, enormous risks, for His power to be displayed. Each time He allows trial in our lives, we must know that **God is risking His glory so His glory can be fully known.**

For it's down there, right there in our lowest points, that we finally lift our eyes high. We are human, and if there's less need for anything else, we become creatures of habit living out our lives on this planet, sometimes unaware there's a battle being fought and a victory to win over the powers that are. That feeling fights with truth, and that truth always wins.

The Leader of the Army allows us to enter battle, to fight alongside Himself. In the depths of our own helplessness, we follow His command. In our shattering, we lift our eyes to His healing.

And when our eyes are lifted high because we would be destroyed if they gazed low, we find truest life. We find Him to be *The Life*, the Alpha and Omega, Beginning and End, of all true joy. Ultimate truth that never dies, and love that always wins.

This, my friends, is why we can trust in a God of truth. Why we can hold on to truth when all else seems louder and perhaps even clearer. Truth may seem dim, but in reality, it never is.

My son felt afraid as I asked him to walk, but truth was, Mama knew something he didn't, and he believed in that truth. He obeyed, and he was blessed.

"Father, thank you that we get to trust you, though you slay us or prosper us. Help us to trust as Job did, long before he was aware of the test you were giving him."

DAY 35

"If you abide in my word, you are truly my disciples, and you will know the truth, and the truth will set you free." John 8: 31b–32, ESV

Living with purpose means we know there is purpose to each circumstance in our lives, whether good or bad. We live by truth.

Here are some truths to speak over our lives today:

When I feel the pain of mistreatment, I listen to God's truth that forgiveness sets me free from bitterness. By listening to truth, I am no longer destroyed by anything that happens to me. I experience cleansing from my own sin because our Father forgives us "as we forgive our debtors" (Matthew 6:12).

When I feel like I can't handle something, I trust that "I can do all things through Christ who strengthens me." When I trust, an Invisible Strength courses through me and I know where my Source lies. I can only trust like that *when there is nothing else to fall back on, and there is no other option but Jesus.*

When I have feelings of self-hatred, I remember that I am "fearfully and wonderfully made" for God's own glory and pleasure. Who am I to fret over what I perceive to be imperfections?

When I feel worthless, I remember that, to my Father, I am worth the life of His Son. *My quest for love ends the moment I believe how much I am already loved and valued.*

When I want more possessions than I have, I know instead that "Godliness with contentment is great gain." I focus on what I do have, and suddenly see myself as one of the most blessed people on earth.

When I idolize any person, I remember that "there is only One good," and that is our Father in heaven. Any human will let me down. I remember to give glory where it is due.

When I feel jealousy rising over something another possesses, I remember to rejoice in all goodness, talent, and beauty wherever it is seen because it is God's heart to show His glory everywhere. *Anything of value in someone else is a showcase of God's own beauty.*

When I feel "less than" any other person, I remember that God created me, and in Him lies all significance. Goodness or perceived greatness on earth should only draw our hearts upward to the Source. *He displays it here, to draw our hearts there.*

When I fear death, I remember that "There is no fear in love" (1 John 4:18), and "Precious in the sight of the Lord is the death of His saints" (Psalm 116: 15). I know that "For me to live is Christ and to die is gain" (Philippians 1:21).

When the world says I need a nicer car, I listen to God's truth of contentment in all things. *I know my value is not based on what I own.*

When my heart recoils at being corrected or rebuked, I listen to God's truth in Proverbs, which says a wise man hears rebukes and becomes wiser for it. Only a fool hardens his heart (Proverbs 1:5).

When I want to eat anything I want whenever I want, I listen to what I know is true, that God created my body with certain needs. He also designed food in a certain way to nourish us. Eating for emotional needs only makes us more depressed as we now have health issues or added pounds to deal with on top of everything else.

When I feel stress in my normal "Mommy world," I remind myself that I am doing exactly what I want to do most. Any vocation has challenges. As I embrace truth, I find myself overjoyed by the simplest things. My times away from it all are even better because I'm drenched in truth while I'm home, and truth affects my soul, my mothering, my everything.

When the world says that women who follow their husband's lead are placing themselves at a lower level of value, I smile inside as I remember that Adam was lonely and incomplete without a helper who was suitable for him. I know that women are the most beautiful creatures God created, and men would cease to thrive if they didn't exist. Just because my role is different doesn't mean it is any less.

When I feel like a trial will never end, I remember that all things do come to an end. Most things change in time, and if they never do, this time on earth is still short in comparison to eternity. Our joy is not dependent on circumstances. As Corrie Ten Boom says, "There is no pit so deep where God's love is not deeper."

When I feel condemnation, and cannot come to God in faith for my sins for fear that I have not "done it right," I remember that Jesus shedding His blood for me was the most perfect thing ever done, and it was done for me. I don't need to "do it right" because He is my perfect sacrifice.

When I fear the aging process in my body, I remember that my values are different than the world's. "The silver-haired head is a crown of glory, if it is found in the way of righteousness" (Proverbs 16:31, NKJV).

When I feel like I cannot endure a trial any longer, I remember that I'm surrounded in a bubble of protection by God's love. Nothing on earth or in Hell can destroy me. Whatever I perceive to be destructive to my well-being and happiness, God turns into something for my good and growth. But only if I listen to His promise. "We know that all things work together for good to those that love God, to those who are the called according to His purpose" (Romans 8:23, NKJV).

When we refuse to follow our fear and listen instead to what God says, we discover more, more, and more freedom.

It's time to discover deep inner joy by allowing God's truth to set us free!

"Lord, help us not to walk in clouds of our own making any longer. Help us to toss lies aside and make way for truth to change our lives."

DAY 36

"My sheep hear My voice, and I know them, and they follow Me."
John 10:27, NKJV

Seattle, one of America's greatest cities, held our family captive by its wonder yesterday. We snapped photos the entire day, enjoying the sight of massive, elaborate structures and elegantly displayed gardens.

The culture of Seattle is different than the culture of our smaller town on the Olympic Peninsula. American culture is vastly different than the cultures in Africa, where my sister lives and raises her family. Her twin lives in Canada with her six girls, and still another sister currently stays in Greece surrounded with Muslim culture. I am soon to travel to Pennsylvania, where I will be drenched in Amish culture.

Cultures may swirl around us but God's love hovers over us.

I wonder why we as Christians subconsciously assume that we can fit in today's culture. Why we don't want to be different. Why we allow and foster an attitude in our kids that to stand out is shameful and undesirable whereas popularity is a thing to be pursued, grasped, and enjoyed.

If we were to travel overseas, maybe we wouldn't mind

standing out because we might not like what surrounds us as much as we love our home country.

We forget that America isn't home, either. Fellow Christians, we are not home, yet.

In the same way we are fine standing out in other cultures, we need to be fine standing out here. Jesus says when we are persecuted, we are blessed, for the kingdom of heaven is ours (Matt. 5:10).

Let's take note of two separate kingdom operations and choose our side distinctly. Let's remember that Jesus also said we cannot be friends of both, and "If anyone loves the world, the love of the Father is not in him" (1 John 2:15b, NKJV).

Let's also remember that the things we tell ourselves are often based on the world's opinion, not Christ's. When we turn to Christ's view on things, our lives change from the inside. We carry a strength and confidence greater than anyone finds by fitting into their culture.

Culture buzzes, swirls, turns, and changes. Women of purpose are bent on finding out what God says to them, and living by unchanging values. Let's rejoice in our calling and call our children to hold God's truth as the most precious thing they will ever find.

While cultures have opposing values, God's values are meant to determine each one and unite us in a common cause.

"And the rain descended, the floods came, and the winds blew and beat on that house; and it did not fall, for it was founded on that rock" (Matthew 7:25, NKJV).

"Lord, as your people, help us see clearly that we cannot be taken with the world and its thoughts more than with yours. Help us build our lives on the Rock, and leave sandy foundations to other builders."

Day 37

"Jesus answered, 'Most assuredly, I say to you, "unless one is born of the Spirit, he cannot enter the kingdom of God."

"'That which is born of the flesh is flesh, and that which is born of the Spirit is spirit.

"'Do not marvel that I said to you, 'You must be born again.'

"'The wind blows where it wishes, and you hear the sound of it, but cannot tell where it comes from and where it goes.'" John 3:5–8, NKJV

History holds its own charm and we often forget that our forefathers and foremothers were people just like us, full of mistakes and in a culture all their own.

"These were more fair-minded than those in Thessalonica in that they received the word with all readiness, and searched the Scriptures daily to find out whether these things were so" (Acts 17:11, NKJV).

Women of truth hold truth for God's sake. They do not sway or turn aside to cultural pressure or pressure from teens or friends. ***We must not allow culture to define us; rather, God wants to permeate culture through His people.***

Much is lost when we are no longer willing to live by truth. But when we are, much is gained and the world around us is affected for the better.

We fail to uphold truth at all costs because we are afraid. Afraid of being perceived as judgmental, afraid of the world's mockery, afraid of not being liked. We are so afraid of offending others that we blithely pass by the most offensive behavior with quiet lips while the world shouts promotion of the very evil Christ came to conquer.

We forget that Jesus says to expect persecution, and that we're blessed when it happens (Matthew 5:10 and 11, ESV). We forget that He asked us not to expect more than He got when He was here.

We are afraid, but we fear lesser things, and things that won't last. We fear things that will fade, things that have no foundation, people who are human just as we are. Should we not rather fear Him who always is and always will be, whose words never die, and by whom all things exist?

If the world promotes abortion, we must speak against it and, perhaps more important, seek out ways to provide support, education, and options to women to reduce the perceived need or desire for abortions.

Though Christians hold greatest truth, they allow themselves to be rendered most silent. Christ asks us how people will hear unless they've been told (Romans 10:14).

Satan uses fear to hinder the light of truth more than he uses any other tactic. Which of us will be unafraid? Which of us will stand for eternity? And which of us will walk in apathy as lies swirl around us, change culture, and hold the loudest voice in society?

"For whoever is ashamed of Me and My words, of him the Son of Man will be ashamed when He comes in His own glory, and in His Father's, and of the holy angels" (Luke 9:26 NKJV).

When we support lies in the name of love, as in embracing

homosexuality in the name of God when God clearly denounces it (1 Corinthians 6:9), we exchange God's best for the world for our own watered-down version of love for the world.

We must accept God's truth, agree with it, and allow it to determine how we live.

Circumstances change, cultures change, friends and family change, but God's word stands forever. Those who apply truth now reap untold benefit where there could be disaster.

As we live by truth, we bring peace and freedom into all areas of our lives.

The power of women set free by truth is greater than we can imagine.

But just as the power to build and bless is great, so also is the power to tear down and destroy. When women aren't living by truth, they can tear down the walls of their home by charging the atmosphere with all manner of unrest, stress, and dissatisfaction. They can cause aching hearts in their kids, and weary their husbands.

We have so much power, so much influence.

Never underestimate the power and purpose of women living by truth!

"Father, thank you for giving us something solid to hold on to in a changing world."

Day 38

"We are afflicted in every way, but not crushed; perplexed, but not driven to despair; persecuted, but not forsaken; struck down, but not destroyed.

"Always carrying in the body the death of Jesus, so that the life of Jesus may also be manifested in our bodies" 2 Corinthians 4:8–10, ESV

Our wounds usually come from others. Worse yet, they often come from those within the church.

If we live on props from other people, we'll be devastated when we face criticism. The part of our brain that activates when we have physical pain also activates when we experience rejection or emotional pain.

It's real, friends. ***Living in denial of your pain only increases the damage.*** Agreeing with the lies destroys you. When people live in rejection, their IQ drops, decision-making stalls, and performance declines.

And there they lie, bleeding and without breath. From that place comes a choice. We can agree with destruction or reach out for life. Living in rejection shows displaced confidence whereas overcoming lies with truth shows our trust in Someone higher.

No matter what has been done or said to you, there is truth to combat all of it. Truth allows you to shake lies, belong rather than feel rejected, and prosper in confidence. Healing private rejection is possible when we believe God's open acceptance.

As one lady put it, there is excruciating pain or exquisite joy. We were all born with a great desire for the latter, and when the former happens we gasp for breath and fall flat.

There, on our faces, we learn to tap in to truth that will lift us up.

Which will have the final say, the pain or the joy, lies or truth? Which will you live by?

And will you, like other noble souls who've been through much, allow exquisite joy to overrule excruciating pain?

Exquisite joy is a gift, and a gift must be received. Today, as we reach out to receive God's truth to us, we will be set free. We will find healing. We will walk in grace because grace overrules damage.

In Christ, we are not damaged goods, we are not victims, we are not destroyed.

Because your confidence must be in Christ. Psalm 27:10 says, "For my father and my mother have forsaken me, but the Lord will take me in." Whether your church, spouse, parents, uncle, aunt, or friend has sinned against you, Christ remains stronger than all of them put together.

You must acknowledge your pain, then let go of your pain.

Jesus came to redeem us, not only from our own sin, but from others' sins toward us. He is our safety, our shield, our stronghold. Protecting us from others' sins and failures is part of His redemption plan. We have plans in this life; so does Christ, and one of His greatest plans is to raise you above what came to harm you.

Many times people receive forgiveness of sins, but fail to see the gift of deliverance from sins committed to them. Never, ever does a child of God need to go down with the wound. He may bleed, he may feel near death, but *God's healing salve is much, much more powerful than the sharpest sword.*

If it were not so, we would all be down. If it were not true, we would not be redeemed, for we would merely rejoice in our own salvation as long as others are faithful and kind. In doing so, we would deny the grace Jesus came to offer and agree with the devil in his destruction.

There is nothing fallen that can keep you from rising!

"Father, thank you for allowing any of us to experience exquisite joy. Thank you for healing our pain as well as saving us from our sin."

DAY 39

"Death and life are in the power of the tongue, and those who love it will eat its fruit." Proverbs 18:21, NKJV

Refusing to receive words from the enemy is part of becoming a woman of truth.

People speak, the devil speaks, and God speaks. Who will you choose to listen to?

There will always be voices to discourage you from becoming all God means for you to be. Words that make you feel insecure, inadequate, crushed, defeated, or condemned are not coming from God.

Listen only to words from the Lord, and refuse to take wrong words in, including the ones in your own mind, which can be some of the worst. It's so easy to believe that we will never be who we are meant to be, that we will never be good enough. We listen, listen, listen to those doubts until we are dragged into the dirt and can barely lift our heads.

Jesus lifts our heads, when before, we buried our faces. Christ clears our countenance, when before, nothing was clear.

When we finally learn to say "No" to all lies, we find clouds clearing above our heads. The lie enters our mind, and just as quickly it leaves because we counter it with truth. Say, in your heart or out loud, "I refuse to receive this."

For those in the habit of receiving lies, it may take many, many times of refusal before you are in the habit of receiving truth alone. Negative habits develop slowly but you can put them away surely.

You may be saying, "But what I feel is true. I am a failure." Or "I have a right to be hurt." We truly have failed and we do have valid reasons for pain. But didn't Jesus have something better in mind than for us to be destroyed by our own failure or someone else's sin? He loves us far too much for that!

Is that not that why Jesus came, to redeem failure and make it new? To cleanse the worst sin and give life? We honor Him when we receive His gift and quit giving the devil opportunity to win.

Counter your own lies with God's truth.

God never condemns; He delivers.

God never puts you down; He lifts you up.

God never holds a grudge after you've repented; He removes the transgression as far as the East is from the West, washes you in His blood, and clothes you in white garments.

God never says you're not good enough; He says His grace is perfected in your weakness. In other words, your weakness is actually an asset to Him because it causes His grace to shine brighter.

God never demands that you perform better; He gives His love so overwhelmingly that it causes you to reflect it from the inside out.

God never judges you from the outside; He sees your heart, and whether or not it is pure.

God never gives you more than you can bear; in fact, His yoke is easy and His burden is light.

God doesn't judge your worth by the number of friends you have; Jesus chose to hang out with those who were rejected by society.

God never thinks more highly of you when you have wealth; Jesus had nowhere to lay His head, and did not seek material gain or repute.

God never compares you with others; He tells you that you are fearfully and wonderfully made by Him, for His pleasure.

God never wakes you up with thoughts of dread for the day; He says His mercies are new each morning. Each day with Him, no matter how difficult, holds the promise of love, purpose, and meaning.

God never, ever makes you feel defeated; He reaches out His hand and lifts you up. Then He turns your sin or mess-up around to create something beautiful.

God never tells you your life is for nothing; even if all you see is ashes, He says He will make beauty out of ashes.

God never makes you feel alone; He says He will never leave you or forsake you.

God never makes you feel purposeless; He says His plans have been there for you from the foundation of the world.

God never turns away; He tries to tell you how much He sees and cares for you by letting you know He sees a sparrow when it falls. Most people are not that fond of sparrows, which is probably why this bird is used for His example. If God sees a sparrow and cares for it, how much more does He care for you?

God never makes us feel overwhelmed; He promises strength for anything that lies ahead.

God never bogs us down with our past; He puts it behind, and asks us to reach forward.

God never measures our worth with bodily perfection; He doesn't see as people see, and looks for the heart.

God never measures us by our popularity or lack thereof; He often seeks out the lowly to perform His greatest tasks. He can only bless the humble and those who will give Him all credit. Popularity has a way of inflating the human mind with its own worth. Is this why Jesus chose many fishermen, shepherds, and lowly tribesmen with whom to spend His time on Earth?

God never depresses us; rather, the gift of His spirit is joy.

Does anyone feel a cloud lifted already? The power of truth is so incredibly life changing, which is why our enemy works overtime to get us to listen to the counter.

Pursue truth, refuse lies, delivered by your own mind or other people, and you will find one burden after another lifted from your shoulders.

"But He answered and said, 'It is written, "Man shall not live by bread alone, but by every word that proceeds from the mouth of God.' "

When you tune in to truth you will begin to wonder where you've been. You will see that you've been so used to listening to the false that you had no idea how wonderful it is to live in truth.

The most wonderful thing is, truth is not contingent on what someone else thinks of you. Truth is always truth. *When God speaks, you cannot argue.*

And when you finally refuse to argue, *you will hear His song more than the devil's lies.*

"You shall know the truth, and the truth shall make you free" (John 8:32, NKJV).

"Father, help us to tune in to your song for our lives."

DAY 40

"Trust in the Lord with all your heart; do not depend on your own understanding." Proverbs 3:5, NIV

I donned the flowered bog boots over my wool socks, grabbed my Bible, and headed down the pasture.

The morning had been filled with school and laundry. A counter of dishes towered high while we tackled math and the six-year-old slowly sounded out words in his "Joan and the Toad" story.

And then, of course, there were leftovers for lunch (because no mama can cook lunch and homeschool at the same time), and the dark chocolate avocado pudding set my palate at ease almost as much as my walk down to the lowlands set my heart aright.

A girl should never wear pink jeans while slipping down a muddy bank. But today, I'm determined enough to find a quiet spot that staining those jeans doesn't seem to matter.

Here, where water washes the shore often enough to coat rocks and uprooted trees with things of the wider sea; here, where birds sing freely and not a soul is in sight, I find what I'm looking for.

Sometimes, a girl needs to unclutter her world in order to unclutter her heart. Because life happens, and things you never expected remain in front of your sight, blocking vision. You strain your neck to see around, but can't; you try glasses of all shades, but vision remains less than clear, and the daunting rock you've been trying to move refuses to budge.

It's just there. We heave, push, and sigh—it doesn't budge and won't even allow us to carry it away.

But God—He's just here, too.

The rocks say it, the birds sing it, all of nature proclaims it, that God is, and He's here, and He's not only here, but He's here *for me*.

I may not buy freedom of soul with my own country's currency, like I buy milk and eggs and boots, but God has His own currency, and it buys me—actually, *gives me*—freedom.

Faith in Him allows me to receive His care, goodness, and love right beside the rock that won't move. I'm an ambassador in a foreign country, and I don't use this country's currency for kingdom goods that only heavenly faith can buy.

It's only when we forget that the soul can only be bought with heavenly currency—in fact, has already been bought for us—that we lose out. We shop in the worst places when we keep scanning the aisles of the world for things that don't exist, things that cannot be bought with our own efforts, things that only the heavenly currency of faith can bestow on our hearts.

Here in the lowlands with unbroken stillness all around, I find again the richness of heaven. Barnacles crunch under my feet, and I know that just as nature brings to me God's unspoken beauty, so I am to bring to my world God's spoken Word, only made available to me by an otherworldly source.

I lean over the rock, and His word speaks life. Unfiltered, real. All the gifts of heaven.

And I wonder why I've been trying to purchase my heart

needs with earthly currency when Heaven purchases so much more.

Ambassadors depend on their country of origin for their needs rather than the currency of the country they are working in. And we, when our souls are barren and dry, must ask ourselves, *what currency are we using to purchase soul desires?*

The pink jeans are stained, and the rock still remains in front of me when I so desperately want to throw it away.

But I can see clearly once again.

I pull myself up the slope with tight grips on weeds that could snap any minute. But my heart that was ready to snap, remains still.

I finally used the currency of my country of origin for the things my heart desired. No frantic shopping that wore me out as I ran here and there—just a quiet walk down to the lowlands with worn, faded, bog boots and pink jeans. Just a heart ready to receive God's word that is always sure to come when we finally use the currency He's given us.

I think this time, I shopped at the right place. I'm satisfied—and who knows, the God Who gives me vision in spite of the rock placed directly in front of me, *may just remove the rock as well.*

If not, He promises to help me scale it, fly right over it, soar above it. Today, that's all I need to know.

John says, "I can do nothing on my own. As I hear, I judge, and my judgment is just, because I seek not mine own will but the will of Him Who sent me."

"The testimony that I have is greater than that of John" (John 5:30 and 36, ESV).

Soul in hard places, you may follow what you think, you may follow after people and what they advise you, but your soul will never truly be at rest until you follow what God says to you.

John was a burning light, and people were willing to follow him for a while, but when Jesus came along, He was even better, and John faded into the background (John 5:35).

Ladies, what is God saying to you right now in your very situation? Is He asking you to forgive, when you have every "right" to be bitter? Is He asking you to be strong, when your weakness threatens to disannul his strength?

May I assure you that if God is asking you to endure, you will find more life right where you are than if you tried everything else and escaped your trial? Heavenly currency is not spent on the easy thing as much as it purchases peace that passes understanding in your hardest thing.

If you are willing to follow Him, you will be rich with gifts that earthly wisdom won't buy for you. Remember to walk with heaven and use its currency for things money can't buy!

"Father, thank you that when I use your resources,
I always walk away full."

DAY 41

"And you will feel secure, because there is hope; you will look around and take your rest in security." Job 11:18, ESV

My four-year-old son was distraught. And for some odd reason I held him in my arms and said, "David, you will see the goodness of the Lord in the land of the living."

"No!" he sobbed.

"What? You don't want to see the goodness of the Lord?" I asked.

"No."

"But you will, David."

He suddenly and violently flung himself into my arms and cried out, "Jesus is playing with my balloon!"

David had received a special balloon, and, as is wont to happen, lost it to the sky. In his four-year-old mind he pictured Jesus in the heavens somewhere, enjoying his lost treasure. And he resented it.

I assured him that his balloon was not being held by Jesus, and that it had indeed floated around the air until it deflated and dropped to the ground somewhere.

As I penned his little story into my journal, a whole new lesson formed in my mind.

How many times do we as adults hesitate to give it all up to the Lord because we picture Him withholding from us our highest joy? Taking from us what we really need? Not caring about our deepest longings? Asking us to give too much in return for too little?

We hold back out of fear that our needs will not be met. That we really know how to orchestrate life better than He does. We must see, instead, that God takes what seems good so there's room for the actual good.

Why would God take from us those we love most dearly?

Why would a dearly loved brother suddenly disappear, never to return again?

Why do those we love most endure trials we wish we could take away, but are helpless to do so?

It seems a contradiction that God takes from us what we think we need in order to show Himself more beautiful. That when we are stripped of it all, His presence becomes even more delightful. That His glory shines more brightly in darkness; that *the very presence of want becomes an opportunity for His fullness to satiate.*

And thus it remains that God is such a friend that He is willing to allow His children trials in order for them to become most satisfied. To show them that nothing in life satiates the soul like He does. It is only that we grope about in our humanness to find what only He can give.

Sometimes He takes our props so we find Him to be the pillar. He knows we need a strong, lasting pillar much more than a few fading props. In light of eternity and the depth of our own hearts, He remains, in spite of it all, the Source of Highest Love because only Love knows how to give, just like that.

"He is no fool who gives what He cannot keep to gain what he cannot lose."—Jim Elliot

"Father, thank you that you never ask us to give
something up without returning blessing on us.
Thank you that we never give in vain."

DAY 42

"Fear not, stand firm, and see the salvation of the Lord, which He will work for you today. For the Egyptians whom you see today, you shall never see again." Exodus 14:1, ESV

"The Lord will fight for you, and you have only to be silent."
Exodus 14:14, ESV

We often don't realize the painful growth that has taken place in a person's life.

So often, testimonies sound grand, almost graceful. Biographies shout of victories in faithful lives. We are awed, as we should be. These are works of grace.

What we do not always see is the day-to-day growth. The trial must come before victory can be shouted. A life must be lived before a biography can be written. Day by day by day, God desires to write *His* story through our lives.

If we say yes, if we are faithful in small things, the purpose of God will be fulfilled. If, however, we are lax and unfaithful, the story God wanted to write about His love in our lives will never be written.

Each moment, each day, each week calls us to pull forth the best of grace because we serve a grace-filled God.

We must embrace the trial in order to learn God's grace. If

we refuse to walk through the valley we will never end up on the mountain. If we never end up on the mountain, who will tell of His grace?

When our lives are said and done, or rather, long before our lives are over, will we have a story? "And they overcame him by the blood of the Lamb and by the word of their testimony, and they did not love their lives to the death" (Revelation 12:11, NKJV).

Testimonies are some of the most powerful means God uses to show His grace to the world.

God does not promise an easy way; He promises grace to travel. Sometimes trials hit us that take our breath away, and it takes every ounce of faith to say "yes" to the Lord. Though God allows trials, He also says we are being changed into His same image, from glory to glory.

This is the secret to walking through trials, *this glory part.* When we do not see the glory to glory, we faint inwardly at the mountain. When we feel that deep exultation even through a strong trial, we are able to smile through tears because we know in the end it will work for our good.

All things, God says, work for the good. *We are in a win/ win situation—as long as we follow the Lord with a "yes."*

God's children can walk through massive trials with a certain calm about them. *There's this victory glint on the sword,* and the shield of faith is able to protect us from all fiery darts.

The victory was already won at the cross when the Son of Man gave His life to redeem and to protect. He won.

Trust Him, and He will win for you, over and over and over again. As he said to Joshua in the face of myriads of ene-my soldiers, "*Stand still*, and see the salvation of the Lord . . ." (Exodus 14:13, NKJV).

It's complex, this standing still. It is otherworldly, a concept unknown to anyone who has not tasted the strength of the Lord.

In the world, everyone fights. Women fight against age, men fight for power, armies fight for peace, children fight for their rights. And in spiritual warfare, we too, want to fight. But it is not until we cease fighting in our own strength that we win.

In this spiritual battle, to fight is to believe in His power, His ability to work for us, in us, through us.

So when you feel all a mess and don't know which way is up or down, when you fear you will fall, breathe a prayer of thanks to the Lord for having won the battle for you. Then step aside, out of the way, and wait on Him to work.

You will find this fight bearable. You will know what Jesus meant when He said, "For my yoke is easy and my burden is light" (Matthew 11:30, NKJV). It's a whole new strategy, but one that works, for "the just will live by faith."

Faith is the avenue through which God's Spirit can work. Trust allows God to step forward. So take courage, friends, and allow yourself to *"stand still and see."*

"Father, help us to cease our striving and to stand still so we see the salvation you've come to offer."

DAY 43

"But those who wait on the Lord will renew their strength." Isaiah 40:31, ESV

We often berate ourselves for not having more courage. Let's take a look at one of the most highly esteemed men of God who ever lived.

Moses lacked courage even after God appeared to him in a burning bush. God spoke to him, directly and clearly, yet he still didn't believe he was up to the job God was calling him to. In Exodus chapter four we see Moses begging God not once, but three times, for a way out of the task of leading thousands of people from a brutal king to another land.

First he says, "But suppose they will not believe me or listen to my voice; suppose they say, 'The Lord has not appeared to you'" (Exodus 4:1, NKJV). The Lord shows him visible signs for the second time. This time, instead of a burning bush, he got to see a staff turn into a serpent and a hand turn leprous, then whole again.

After all that, Moses still says, "Oh, my Lord, I am not eloquent, either before nor since you have spoken to your servant, but I am slow of speech and slow of tongue" (Exodus 4:10, NKJV). To this the Lord replies, "Who has made man's mouth? Or who makes the mute, the deaf, the seeing, or the blind? Have not I, the Lord? Now therefore, go, and I will be with your mouth, and teach you what you shall say" (Exodus 4:11–12, NKJV).

Moses must have been incredibly afraid for he still said, "O, my Lord, please send by the hand of whomever else You may send" (Exodus 4:13, NKJV).

After this, the Lord's anger was kindled, but he had mercy on his shy, ineloquent servant, and said, "Is not Aaron, the Levite, your brother? I know that he can speak well. And look, he is also coming out to meet you. When he sees you, he will be glad in his heart. Now, You shall speak to him and put the words in his mouth. And I will be with your mouth and with his mouth, and I will teach you what you shall do. So he shall be your spokesman to the people. And he himself shall be as a mouth for you, and you shall be to him as God. And take this rod in your hand, with which you shall do the signs" (Exodus 4:14–17, NKJV).

Do you see this patriarch of the faith? This man God spoke to audibly, appeared to with signs, and on the mountain gave a tablet written with his own words. He spent days with the Lord and reappeared to the people with his face so bright with God's presence they covered him with a veil.

Moses, the friend of God, one of the best who ever lived, was scared out of his mind.

Notice how he spoke with the Lord. He didn't deny his fear, but expressed it until he was assured. Only then did he have courage to move.

Notice also the Lord's patience. He didn't move on to someone else, but gave him signs and encouragement to reassure him. He even sent another man to help him do the most difficult part.

Moses hated public speaking and he wasn't good at it. But in all Moses' hesitancy, *God still needed and wanted to use him.*

Moses didn't push himself, berate himself, or rush ahead without courage, but he did talk with God.

Many times we do the opposite—we condemn ourselves for needing more courage while we push and rush ahead to do what we think God wants us to do. But we don't stand still and speak to our Father until He gives us the tools or wisdom or assistance we need.

He promises that those who wait on Him shall ". . . renew their strength; they will mount up with wings as eagles, they shall run and not be weary, they shall walk and not faint."

Friends, He wants us to wait, to stand still, to listen, to pour out our hearts, and to hear His answer. He will speak, and His words will bring stillness and courage in the face of all odds, including our own sin and weakness.

He is not a God who pushes you when you're afraid, but a Father who leads you out of your fear. And He invites you to converse with Him, just as you invite your children to speak to you about their fears.

Talking with God is the most effective means of reducing fear and gaining courage.

"Lord, thank you that you want to use us in spite of ourselves, and when we see our weakness, you walk us into strength."

Day 44

"There is no fear in love, but perfect love casts out fear." 1 John 4:18, ESV

I put on the bulky blue life jacket and stood, still wary, in the middle of the sparkling blue lake waters.

I wasn't just afraid of the water, I was feeling silly. Stupid, rather. Standing there like some child while adults and children alike splashed all around. Thank goodness I had an excuse — my five-year-old stood with me, and he had a bright blue cast on his arm.

Hopefully, they would all think he was the reason for my hesitancy to dive under. But I knew the life jacket gave me away.

Why was I afraid? Afraid of water, afraid of what others thought of me. When would I cease to be afraid?

I dunked under, and then, I willed my body down. The jacket held me up, and I swam. It was glorious, even though I wasn't doing it on my own. Over and over again I conquered the panic of a lifelong water paranoia as I tried to draw in my knees to stand up in water only to my waist.

It's amazing how afraid we can be of things that hold no real threat, when we should be more afraid of being threatened by fear itself.

Back on the sandy shore, the sun shone hot, and I pulled out one of my favorite books. Staci Eldredge has a window into the soul of women like I've rarely seen, and she words it beautifully—how we refuse to believe the strength, beauty, and grace the Lord has given us because we are so taken with our wounds.

She tells of Hinduism, where a woman is worth less than a cow; of Islam, where it takes three men to verify her story in court; of China, where, for many years, little girls' feet had been bound; of Africa, where clitoridectomy (female circumcision) is a common practice because sexually aware women are considered dangerous.

Then there's the men who want four wives, but expect their women to have only one husband. Men who beat their wives. Men who view women as property rather than human beings with equal value.

I am a firm believer in divine order in the home, but ladies, our value is no less than a man's, and we don't need to be afraid of our femininity. Perhaps Satan targeted Eve, in part because she had so much capacity for love and beauty.

Satan always targets those of great value while he cares less about people or things that hold no threat.

Do you know, really know, that we are the crown of creation? That we are here because the world was not complete without us?

Why are so many of us insecure and afraid? Why, down through the ages, have women been targeted more than men for misuse and abuse?

If Satan targets us so much with his arrows of fear and insecurity, don't you think it's because he sees the capacity we have to strengthen the world around us with love and trust?

That if we are taken with perfect love, it will cast out all fear (1 John 4:18)?

He tries to fill us with fear so we can't be taken with Perfect Love.

If he makes us afraid of our beauty, don't you think he knows how vital beauty is in this world? (Every woman has beauty to offer. Let me repeat that: *every single woman*.) Women were designed by God to love, appreciate, and cultivate beauty. What is more opposing to the devil's desire for destruction?

Where he destroys, we build. Women were created to build, nurture, bring life.

Ladies, Satan causes us to believe that our greatest asset is our greatest source of shame. He wants us to feel that being a woman—a true, whole, complete woman—is a liability or somehow shameful, rather than a tremendous gift to the world.

Satan tries to convince women that we are not enough the way God created us, that we're missing something, or that the wounds we've experienced have left us permanently damaged. He tries to get us to look to hobbies, accomplishments, relationships, food, or things to fill that vacant spot in our hearts or to distract us from the pain of our wounds.

And then God steps in, giving us Himself in all His breathtaking beauty and reminding us that we are His creation and He makes no mistakes. Relationships and accomplishments and all those other things are often good gifts from God, but the only thing we need to be whole is Him. When we allow anything but God to define us, to give us security, to fill us with confidence, we will live in a perpetual state of striving and neediness, because God created us to depend on Him alone

God may remove the lesser in our lives so we can be filled with the greater. Because when we are distracted with partial filling, we never come to Him for complete fullness. He uses even our wounds to bring us to greater wholeness than if we never had the wound at all.

We can go down with the lies, offenses, hurts. We can agree with them and allow them to have the final say in our lives. *We can be defined by our hurts, or we can be defined by our healing.*

Will you agree with God that there is nothing to fear, because "Perfect love casts out fear?" Will you agree with God that you are a woman created with an important purpose in God's plan? Will you, like so many courageous women before you and all around you, defy darkness and march ahead with the light you were created to share?

"Lord, help us to fulfill our calling by bringing life, beauty, and grace to all those around us."

Day 45

"Whatever you do, work heartily, as for the Lord and not for men, knowing that from the Lord you will receive the reward of the inheritance, for we serve the Lord Christ." Colossians 3:23–24a, ESV

I wrapped my homemade black coat tightly about my waist and stared at those buggy wheels jostling back and forth, waiting for me to climb in. With one quick hop, I scaled the steps into crowded space and sank into the seat while watching Dad hold the reins.

With a powerful neigh, the horse lunged into the air so high I was convinced he would land on his back, on top of the carriage that held Mom and all nine of us kids. Dad had barely made it over the tall, thin wheel before joining us, and his loved horse had all he could take of waiting.

Crash! He landed back on all fours and lunged away at full speed. Dad's arms were taut on the reins, trying to hold him back while white foam slathered out of the horse's mouth and dripped away. Away, and back through the wind to our heads covered in black bonnets, faces bare, open to receive whatever the wind flung at us.

I wondered how his mouth could keep from tearing as he raced down the road, why he had to be so impatient, what drove him out of his senses like that. But Dad kept laughing and had it all under control, flying through the wind with his adventure of a horse.

Dad always had everything under control. He was the hardest working, kindest Daddy a girl could have, and I thought he was wisdom itself. If Dad could manage the horse, we would all be just fine.

But Dad had five kids old enough to drive to school, and they needed a safe horse. He hired a truck driver one day to haul a new, steady horse home for his kids. She was fat; she was slow. But, she was entirely safe enough for us to spend ninety minutes alone on the roads with her each day.

We would yell into thin air to urge her to speed, but her version of speed only lasted a few seconds, and back she was, plod, plod, plod. That long, steep curve of a hill coming up ahead always wore her down to a walk as slow as a turtle.

"Oh," I groaned. "I'm so hungry. Hurry up, Nancy!"

She stopped right before the hill. What on earth?

And then it dawned on me. This fat, lazy, safe, brown horse took my "Oh" for a "Whoa."

I had to laugh in spite of myself, knowing she would stand there for the rest of the day if I let her, as if procrastination would somehow dissolve the hill.

But, it wouldn't. And it never, ever does, not for the horse, and not for us. Willing something difficult away by waiting to do the right thing only prolongs the problem and makes the task even more difficult.

Friends, what is that hard thing in your life today? What has God said to you about it?

If He asks you to trust, and you put off trusting so you can gratify your fear for a while, it will be more difficult to trust in the end. You may also make a mess out of the problem as you release fear into the atmosphere instead of peace.

If God is asking you to hand over that concern of yours, and you keep hanging on to it, worry lines appear on the forehead rather than a radiant countenance from a heart at rest.

If God is asking you to love your spouse with your all, but you gripe one more day, one more month, one more year, before loving with 100 percent rather than 70 percent, you prolong dissatisfaction rather than give birth to new life.

If you know you need to change your diet for health's sake, putting it off until next year denies you the joy of living well, of adding vibrancy to your years.

Procrastination is a habit developed out of fear that taking God at His word will bring less gratification than doing things our own way will.

And there is time for all the good things God wants to do in our lives—we just need to quit squandering our lives.

If we procrastinate long enough, the days turn into years and God still hasn't been able to brush beauty across the canvas of our lives because we insist on standing there wiping mud all over it.

We have our reasons. The pain is too great to release, the emotional gratification from addicting foods too satisfying, the fear too strong to replace with trust. So we live our days by what we feel, and hold off on letting our lives change from the inside out.

But God. He beckons us on, forward, upward, right up that steep hill. Standing before it won't dissolve it, but following God's word to your own heart will help you scale it and reach heights you've only dreamed of. Don't procrastinate, but plunge ahead with full speed and implicit trust in a God who cannot fail.

Nothing good comes without a whole lot of courage, and it won't come unless you step right into it.

"Father, help us not to put off things you are calling us to put on, today, without delay."

Day 46

"Again, the kingdom of heaven is like treasure hidden in a field, which a man found and hid; Then for joy over it he goes and sells all that he has and buys that field.

"Again, the kingdom of heaven is like a merchant in seeking beautiful pearls, who, when he had found one pearl of great price, went and sold all that he had, and bought it." Matthew 13:44–45, NKJV

It was her face. I had never seen such a radiant woman. Yes, she was beautiful, but it was not her beauty that caught me. Joy exuded from her countenance as she introduced herself to me and I watched her mingle with the crowd.

It was infectious.

I got to know her and she became one of my dearest friends. As she opened her life, I discovered that she did not live a perfect, trial-free life. Many times she spoke of difficulties in her way, but joy remained.

I discovered that she was very secure in the Lord and her relationship with Him in spite of the fact that her father abandoned her as a child and wanted nothing to do with her when she sought him as an adult.

I observed her eyes well up with tears as she spoke of Jesus and all He meant to her. I saw her hold on to the Lord when people failed her. I watched as she prayed over difficulties in her life and trusted the Lord instead of trying to work it out on her own.

Fulfilling your divine destiny is joy with no comparison even when others don't fulfill theirs. My friend's father obviously wasn't—*but she could, anyway.*

We often fall short of all we are offered. We become lax and don't experience the excitement that comes when we give our all. This is a crying shame, because we are missing out on the abundance Jesus promises—and it hinders others from joining in.

Depression and duty never draw anyone. Joy does!

People hold back parts of themselves for fear of losing happiness because they haven't known the full joy from utter abandonment. If we are not full of the Spirit, then yes, trying to be good is a sure cause for depression.

Christianity is not a religion to do; It is a relationship to enjoy.

Jesus is not before us with heaviness to bear; He says His yoke is easy and His burden is light.

He invites the weary to come to Him so they can have rest.

He does not force us to serve Him; rather, we love Him because He first loved us.When He asks us to sacrifice something, it is because He wants to give us something better.

When we are weak, He is strong.

When we would go under, He bears us up and helps us grow instead.

Trying to "do Christianity" without knowing the fullness of the Spirit is a recipe for disaster. If that's where you're at, you are probably more miserable than many people who don't know the Lord at all. If that is the case, take heart—joy waits for you!

At the foot of the cross, in repentance of who you are and all you are, He will find you, and take you there. Find the purpose He created you for, go for it with all you have, and you will know true joy!

"Father, thank you that joy is one of your greatest gifts to women. Help us to receive this gift."

DAY 47

"But the fruit of the Spirit is love, joy, peace, patience, gentleness, kindness, goodness, faithfulness, gentleness, self control; against such things there is no law." Galatians 5:22 and 23, ESV

The sun shone warm over Grevvar Farms as the wagon wheeled slowly across the fields. There's not much more to desire when you're pulled along by two beautiful, black horses on a sunny day.

Country music swelled over the farm while generous men served large slabs of beef to hundreds of hungry people. Eggs were tossed and candy sought in mounds of hay by excited children. I swung freely on the large swing and rode the seesaw with my four children.

Just because I could.

The moon rose in a yellow sliver and my body swayed to the beat of the music. Even the gray heads were dancing, some adept and smooth, all with a smile.

It's good for the soul to have fun.

My ten-year-old son's eyes blazed with energy as he dashed about the dark and climbed on one wagon after another. I'm not sure how he managed to get that watermelon down so quickly in the eating contest, juice squirting out of his mouth, and I'm glad he declined participation in the pie contest.

But in a strange way, I was proud of those girls who got up there to see how quickly they could down a piece of pie. Whipped cream all over their mouths, they let go of the need to impress, and chose rather to be blessed.

Though I declined joining the pie contest that night, in my soul was a deep capacity for joy and happiness that used to be foreign to me. I used to be bound up tight, wound up tight, with a load of *something*. I didn't even know what all it was, but I knew I wasn't free like the people I admired.

I was codependent, so taken with others that I couldn't find my own way out of the haze to clarity. So taken with myself that I was unable to be taken with Christ. I was largely dependent on people for my joy, security, and love, and therefore missed out on the gifts of Christ.

Even just this week, as I prayed about something weighing on me, I realized afresh how much I myself was contributing to the problem. My new prayer became, "Lord, I just want to be healthy. Let me be whole."

Let me focus on my own wholeness more than that of others. Because when we worry about that other upset person, we end up even more upset. When we try so hard to fix things out of our control, we end up with minds out of control. We become so obsessed, consumed with problems around us that we never find the way out of our own issues. Friends, let me assure you, as long as you're consumed with other people—their approval, their attention, or even their needs—you will never find your own personal freedom. The only path to freedom is by being consumed with Christ.

When Christ planned your life, He never planned your freedom or joy to be contingent on another.

We must learn to let go. Letting go includes our parents, church, spouse, friends, kids' friends, and the world. This doesn't mean we don't care; it does mean we find life, and only those with abundant life will be able to share it with others.

Only those with their own peace draw others who need peace.

I stood by the fire, watching couples sway to the music. The band was good, so good I was loath to leave, even with five dusty kids still needing to get to bed. We all need to find opportunities like this to let it all go and *have fun.*

We don't need to head to unhealthy places to have fun; our kids shouldn't need to leave home to find it. Here, now, today, when we cease depending on others, we find joy, find our hearts swaying to the beat of better, greater, deeper things.

How is it that Christians become so burdened with living "right" that they end up barely living?

How is it that we depend on others so much that we become someone no one can depend on?

How is it that the very problems we are determined to solve end up destroying us, because we've not let go?

Problems can be thrown on God, who knows how to carry them. You cannot save your child, but you will draw him closer to Christ when you learn to live freely in God's love. You may not be able to change your child, but you can allow this very salvation to permeate the atmosphere he or she lives in. But you can only do that when you refuse to be destroyed by the things concerning you.

God is the mover, changer, saver of the universe. We are not. When we find ourselves obsessed with others, even obsessed with changing or helping them, we become controlled by the very thing we long for them to shed. We must be taken with greater things.

If you want to draw the soul of your child, give him something to be drawn to.

Today, dare to be free, dare to shed your weight, dare to pray rather than push, release the burden more than carry it, find your life in Christ more than in others. Dare to believe you were destined for joy and allow your heart to sway to the beat of it!

You will become one of those drawing others in, rather than one pushing others out and wondering why. You will bear the light, and give light.

"Father, help us to live in freedom,
and bring that freedom to others."

DAY 48

"I am the resurrection and the life.

"Whoever believes in me, though he die, yet shall he live, and everyone who lives and believes in me shall never die." John 11:25 and 26, ESV

I think back to the time in my own life where I was anything but joy-filled. In crowds, I was self-conscious to the point of being consumed. I lacked confidence in every way and my countenance showed my suffering.

As I grew in the Lord and became secure in Him, I became freer. People remarked to me often that I had changed and become so much more beautiful. I would smile, thank them, and feel deep gratitude for the Lord's working in my life.

A joy-filled woman inspires young and old alike. *And may I encourage you ladies that soul joy is possible whether or not your life is easy?*

Soul joy comes from knowing how much the Lord loves you and how great His plan is for you. It comes from seeing who He is to you and for you. Joy is from God Himself, and I believe when we enter heaven there will be an abundance of joy such as we have never seen or felt on this earth.

Adam and Eve had nothing but joy in the Garden. Delight

over God's creation in each other, in God, and the beautiful world in which they lived. The devil deceived them into seeking more joy by tasting forbidden fruit, and thus, as has happened for thousands of years since, striving for their own happiness outside of God's will brought grief and disaster.

Though joy was stolen in one day, Christ returns it to us every day.

If you ponder things that steal your joy, you will see they are all a result of the fall. Our lives are affected by sin in the world. We hurt. We cry. We feel the pain of mistreatment. We grow tired. So did Eve after the angel sent them out of the Garden and guarded the entrance with a flaming sword.

We are daughters of a fallen woman. *But more than that, we are daughters of a redemptive king!*

Our king has come back to restore the life that the Devil stole that day in the Garden. He has come to bruise the head of the serpent. Though people and circumstances of a fallen nature surround us, He has come to restore our joy.

This is why my friend, who has her share of trials, radiates joy everywhere she goes. She has found Him who heals her heart, makes all things work for good in her life, and restores to her the years the locusts have eaten. She knows that walking in freedom from Satan's curse on the world brings inner healing to our hearts and sets us free to enjoy life and live to the fullest, regardless of the effects of the curse surrounding our lives.

When our inner being is healed by our Father, we are set free to love life and people as never before. To know delight and wonder over small, minute things in the day. To worship freely before a great and good God, to laugh from way down deep because we are able to love, and live fully right where we are.

More than being happy with your circumstances, joy is the settled assurance that God is in control of every detail of your life, the quiet confidence that everything is going to be all right, and the determined choice to praise God in every situation.

With that interpretation of joy, no one is left behind.

"Lord, thank you that joy is all-inclusive."

DAY 49

"For godly sorrow produces repentance leading to salvation, not to be regretted; but the sorrow of the world produces death." 2 Corinthians 7:10, NKJV

How do we deal with the pain of regret? Know this: God has a plan for you, regardless of your past.

Living in despair over your past is a result of not truly accepting the forgiveness, grace, and joy Christ came to give. Repentance always leads to salvation. Living in regret leads to depression and a sense of uselessness.

Intense sorrow for sin is healthy and good, even needful at times, but if you place your trust in Christ, you will find a deep inner healing and burden lifted.

Walking in regret, however, is a burden too heavy to bear. Jesus came to set you free from your past.

Repentance lifts your guilt; living in regret keeps you in shame.

Choose to accept the beautiful plan God has for you, today. Allow Jesus to take that regret on His own shoulders as He promised to do. Deliverance from regret is part of God's plan of redemption for you.

There is joy in spite of the mess.

You may have had huge setbacks, your life may have gotten messy, your children may have failed you or others. Your friends may have seen your bad side and you may have needed to ask for forgiveness. Your finances may be in bad shape. You may have health issues.

Some of you may be facing things much, much more difficult than any I have mentioned here.

Life gets messy.

We enter the adult world eager to experience all the good things life has to offer. We shy away from difficult situations. We dream big.

But what if we mess up? What if, instead of having a flowing source of income, we are getting further into debt? What if we've hurt our loved ones or been hurt so badly we feel totally derailed?

And what happens inside of us when the mess is visible to those around us and our perceived reputations go south?

If you find your joy gone, you may be assured you've been looking for it in the wrong places. *Joy is a fruit of the spirit, not a fruit of a perfect life.*

Joy is not conditional like happiness is. Walking with Jesus guarantees a sure and deep joy simply because He gives us that gift.

His mercy is real. His gift is free. It is always available, even after we discover that life brings more than enough trial, or we didn't perform like we believed we would. Instead of feeling amazing about ourselves or our lives, we are humbled and drawn to the cross.

Because the cross is where He wants us, after all. And if, in the process of bringing us there, He allows us to be humbled and tried, we still find surest joy and He gets all the praise.

Circumstantial happiness has little need for a Savior. But when life gets messy and we find joy for what joy is, the Savior's worth is magnified.

Joy is a gift to all. Live it up!

"Father, bring us to the cross as the surest beginning place for joy."

DAY 50

"On the last day of the feast, the great day, Jesus stood up and cried out, 'If anyone thirsts, let him come to me and drink.

" 'Whoever believes in me, as the scripture has said, "Out of his heart will flow rivers of living water."'" John 7:37–38, ESV

Life is not so much about being loved as it is about loving. Not so much about being admired as about praising the One worthy of all admiration.

Life is more about filling our hearts with worship than it is about filling our lives with people who make us feel great about ourselves.

Life is good when we realize that joy is free. No one owes us happiness, but joy comes when we realize we get to have it no matter what.

Our hearts are created to soar.

A gift is always free. We often see suffering people who are full of grace, and blessed people who are living in misery. If joy wasn't free, only those with seemingly perfect lives would get to experience it. If joy wasn't free, others would get to steal it from you. If joy wasn't free, we would keep trying to hold all things unpleasant at bay.

We would succumb to grasping for happiness instead of receiving joy.

Because joy is free, all of us get to share in it. All of us get to live it, hold it, revel in it. Joy brings us to redemption from things that drag us down and would destroy us.

Life is not so much about surrounding ourselves with happiness as it is realizing that joy surprises us at every turn once we finally cease trying to perfect everything (and everyone) around us so we get to live a happy life.

We begin finding pleasure in the smallest things. We sigh with contentment even though others would wonder why. When we let go of perfection in people or places, we get to experience perfect Love in each place of our lives.

Life is rich and full once we cease grasping and accept the gift. Your friends or spouse are free from your expectations to bring happiness to you. No one earns this for you. Jesus hands it to you as from Himself.

There's no need to bob up and down in the waters of your own fulfilled and unfulfilled expectations. Instead, hold on to the gift of God's joy, which you didn't earn, nor did others earn it for you. And when you feel its worth, you will be loath to part with it just because something (or someone) failed to make you happy. You are worth more than that, and so is your gift.

Joy is a gift (regardless of circumstances) because the infinite does not rest on the finite.

The finite was created within the infinite. How then can we breathe so deeply of things created and so little of the Creator?

When we are absolutely taken with what always was, presently is, and always will be, we are set free to enjoy the beautiful.

Joy is so much more than a vacation, new dress, perfect date, or awesome friends.

Joy is the soul enamored, enraptured, and set back in awe of a being who spells INFINITY.

The finite melts in light of all He is to the heart. When the Infinite abides, the finite finally sinks to where it belongs and makes way for the soul to rejoice in the higher, greater, better, wiser, and always good.

"Lord, help us to breathe more deeply of you as creator than we do of things created."

DAY 51

─────────────

"To grant to those who mourn in Zion—to give them a beautiful headdress instead of ashes,

"The oil of gladness instead of mourning, the garment of praise instead of a faint spirit;

"That they may be called oaks of righteousness, the planting of the Lord, that He may be glorified." Isaiah 61:3, ESV

I sat in my car watching a lady across from me in the parking lot. She wore a cap on her head and was engrossed in her iPhone, but kept pouring sugar into her mouth, packet after packet, mouthful after mouthful. Her face mirrored depression and I knew only someone desperately in need of solace would sit there pouring that much sugar into her mouth.

What was her life like? Was she one of those who wanted to commit suicide and needed to know someone cared?

I finally decided I had little to lose by checking in on her. I tapped lightly on her window and asked if she was OK. She was embarrassed (of course), and quickly assured me nothing was wrong. I told her I just wanted to check in, and left as quickly as I came. Now two of us were embarrassed! But as I drove away, I realized I showed a lady that someone cared.

Whatever her problem, now she knew someone cared enough to check in. Hopefully it made a difference.

I wonder if she knows Jesus. Thing is, so many who say they know who He is also confess to little joy in their lives. Why, then, is this thing the Spirit wants to give described as a fruit?

Fruit grows naturally on a fruit tree without any striving. In fact, you'd have to try *not* to grow fruit on a fruit tree. I think this is why joy (among so many other things) is described as a fruit of the Spirit.

Where He truly lives, there is joy.

Happiness from great circumstances, or joy because you know God, are two very different things. The former is dependent; the latter, nothing can destroy. You can have joy in spite of tears; joy in daunting trials; joy when life seems to fail you.

This joy is your companion as long as you have His spirit. Feeling Him with you, in you, and for you is comparable to nothing.

I want us to see that sadness over difficult things is different than an overall lack of joy. And sometimes, a lack of joy is compounded by things that need attention, such as chemical imbalances, lack of sleep, an excessive amount of stress, and so forth. If you are in such a place, hang on to God's promises and seek Him for the answers you need, whether they are physical, emotional, or spiritual.

Whatever place you find yourself in, God means to hold you and gift you with peace. This in itself brings joy!

"Father, thank you that you abide with us, in us,
and live joy through us."

DAY 52

"Or do you not know that your body is the temple of the Holy Spirit who is in you, whom you have from God, and you are not your own?" 1 Corinthians 6:19, NKJV

I had tasted of Christ, and wanted more. But then I heard the phrase "hosting the Presence" and it became my favorite. Perhaps because I love hospitality.

One of my aunties is an amazing hostess and helped cultivate that desire in me. When we were kids, we would stay at her house for a week at a time, during which we encountered many little acts of kindness. She would fill baskets of snacks and drink packets close to our bedroom. The beds were comfy and food was always plentiful and delicious. But what warmed me most was her undying care for us. I would see her alone with someone, asking about their well-being. Warmth radiated her soul, and she was the picture of comfort and tenderness. Her home, though less than perfect, held warm touches throughout, and her white Christmas lights lit up the kitchen even when it wasn't Christmas season.

I loved her, and after marriage, I had the same desire to host well. I wanted my doors open, plenty of nourishing food available, and a clean, welcoming atmosphere. I wanted flowers on the porch and Bible verses on the walls. To love on people became one of my greatest desires.

Perhaps this is why the words "hosting the Presence" became real and tangible to me.

To host His presence is to have Him dwelling in you. He dwells in you when you fully and completely release your life to His control, when you trust Him for forgiveness, and ask Him to wash you clean. He keeps dwelling there as you walk by faith in this way, not by trying to be righteous, but by trusting Him to be righteous in you. It is all Him, each step of the way, and you cannot dwell in Him but through faith alone. I used to believe I was saved by faith but would be kept saved through obedience, so I was exhausted.

No matter how many good things I did, I could not win, could not master this sinful nature within me. My works of "obedience" led me further and further from rest in Christ, because no matter how hard I tried to obey, I always fell short.

Trying to do the works of God without the indwelling spirit of God through faith is futile. We must first of all *be* before we can *do*. I came to see that not only was I saved initially through faith, I was also sanctified and kept righteous through faith. When I saw evil in myself, I no longer had to grit my teeth and try harder; I could, instead, reckon myself dead to that sin because of Christ.

I learned to lay my head of the bosom of Christ no matter what I felt, and reckon Him to be greater and victorious. He brought victory and peace from that place of rest.

This, my friends, is true rest. It's the difference between religion and a relationship. The difference between exhausting labor and joy-filled living.

Trusting in that way does not condone sin. Rather, your sin

is taken care of and you are freed from it. *Christ in you can do nothing other than purge you from sin.*

True faith produces good works. It's not the other way around—that good works result in saving faith. If you trust Christ fully, you will obey God because He is in you and He cannot help but be righteous (Romans 6:1 and 11).

Hosting His presence is all about knowing God. "The Spirit Himself bears witness with our spirit that we are children of God" (Romans 8:16, NKJV). If you do not have the witness, seek the Lord earnestly until you do. Believe Him, yield to Him, trust Him with those sins you've never had victory over before. *Though you fail yourself, He will not fail you.*

Right now, simply lay your head on His chest and trust Him with that sin, those problems, those joy stealers. Out of that trust, a relationship will happen that will make you new.

Ask Him to fill you so full of Himself, and then begin hosting Him. What an honor! What a delight! You, we, I, get to host the King of Kings and Lord of Lords. We get to be a temple for Him to dwell in.

When we taste of that fullness and feel His presence, when we know Him as our very best friend, we find what every person on earth is looking for: *joy*! It lasts through trials, weakness, when you suffer wrong, or when there is nothing humanly speaking that would give you joy.

This kind of joy is a fruit because He dwells in you and no one can take it from you.

"Father, thank you for the ultimate gift of your presence."

DAY 53

---

*"Rejoice in the Lord always; again I will say, Rejoice. Let your rea-
sonableness be known to everyone. The Lord is at hand." Philippians 4:4–5, ESV*

My brain swirled in circles as I navigated an hour with Ve-
rizon's tech solution guy. Thank goodness some people
are patient and kind because I'm anything but tech savvy.

He even thanked my husband for being a police officer, and
then, he thanked me for being a cop's wife.

**Some people choose not to be frustrated when they could
be, and to give joy instead.**

I left the phone before we finished because guests were
coming and I was unprepared for two other families to arrive
at the door. Throwing tablecloths, hastily stirring lemonade,
sweeping porches — you know, ladies, those moments when you
want to reach a thousand ways but you're only one person.

My haste ended with a gigantic crash, broken glass, and
sticky liquid dashing over the kitchen. Puddles formed inside
drawers, drenching utensils and dripping through cabinets.

It was one of those moments when you want to cry, but
because you're an adult, you stare in shock for a moment and
then start tackling the mess. My twelve-year-old daughter

rushed in, and with her help, it was under control minutes before the guests arrived.

The guests left at a late hour and my guys went out the door in search of more rats to hunt (our shed is infested) while I crashed for a night's sleep.

The next morning dishes stood on the counter and I was exhausted after a short night. The water jugs were empty, and I took Little Buddy with me to fill them. There, on the mountain, we found joy in sunshine and fresh, clear mountain water hosed straight into those big blue jugs for another two weeks' supply.

There's so much joy to be found right in the middle of mundane moments.

Then there was the laptop to replace, and I could choose to go alone, or invite my daughter along.

Creating joy.

I could have time alone, or I could create a morning to remember. I chose yes instead of no, and she ran off to put on her prettiest summer shirt. She asked for pigtails, those delightful, high ponytails that accent her brown eyes and soft cheeks dented deep with dimples.

We left the house and Little Buddy wanted to go, too. I looked at his stained T-shirt, hesitated, and then said, "Yes, hop in!"

Sometimes we get to choose joy for others, too.

Business was complete, and two little people buckled in the car. I could choose to go home, or create more joy by taking them on a date. I could go home to accomplish more, or sit in the sunshine with my favorites and eat ice cream.

Because what's more delightful than a little boy with a gigantic blue cast on his arm diving into ice cream on a hot day?

Or a dimple-cheeked girl with brown pigtails holding a lem-on-y flavored cone?

Someone left a coffee cup on that outdoor table, old drips dried onto white ceramic. I read the words,

"Enjoy life. Cultivate relationships. Make a difference."

We ate ice cream, talked about the challenge of school coming up, and took selfies just for fun and more memories. Her heart, her life, her thoughts, her happiness in the moment were all stacking up the joy for this mama's heart.

There's so much more to be enjoyed than we give ordinary moments credit for.

And then, because we get to choose joy, we entered a little shop just for fun. There, stacked on shelves, were some of my favorite wall hangings with words just for the moment. They grabbed at the core of me and some sort of raw, brave power rose inside.

"Be the woman that when the devil sees you get up in the morning, he says, 'Oh, no! She's up!'"

"Lord, help us to choose joy, for in doing so we choose you."

Day 54

"For I am persuaded that neither death nor life, nor angels nor principalities nor powers, nor things present nor things to come, nor height nor depth, nor anything other created thing, will be able to separate us from the love of God which is in Christ Jesus our Lord."
(Romans 8:38–39 NKJV)

Waves lapped on the shore that windy, blusterous day. My friend lay fast asleep, overcome with pain, her face pale and her arms white and thin. My eyes filled with tears and I quickly wiped them away. She was a lovely mama of four who wanted to live, but cancer snapped its menacing jaws twice at her very life.

I watched her for three years. This endless battle of a rare type of cancer with no cure. Each time I went to her house, I wondered why she, and not me? What made me live healthy and strong while my dear friend fought so long and hard just to breathe? I had four kids, she had four. My husband was a cop, so was hers. She home schooled, so did I. And on this day, three years later, her colon was partially gone and she lay there, barely able to speak. My heart went still because no emotion could express what I felt for her and those she loved. I left the room in tears and cried my way out of the hospital into sunshine I knew I didn't deserve more than she.

As I left a bread store I had stopped by, I noticed a truck in the parking lot, bright yellow with a honeybee painted on the back. Beside the bee, these powerful words, "O Death, where is your sting?" (1 Corinthians 15:55, NKJV). As I drove farther, a massive rainbow formed over the road. It wasn't a normal rainbow with perfect strips of color, but unusually wide, more like a sunset.

I knew God was speaking to me, and my heart filled with peace. I never see yellow trucks with verses on them defying death's sting, and I never see rainbows (a sign of promise) that wide. The love I felt from my Father filled me with comfort, and in a strange way, with joy.

I have faith that if it were me on that hospital bed, He would be right there, giving peace through tears. He would give joy in an unearthly way. For those who know Christ, even death has lost its sting.

Christ Himself is an all-inclusive, non-exclusive triumph of the soul in which love always wins.

If you hang on, if you seek Him, if you ask for Him, He will reveal Himself to you in this way and you will rest assured that regardless of life's outcome, you will be OK. Until His return, we are part of a messed-up world, but in this world, Christ triumphs. He came not only to redeem you from your sin, but to lift you above your circumstances as well.

You were born to soar.

Do you wonder why Christians in the Roman coliseum sang as their loved ones were torn apart by lions? They knew that love wins. They knew death has been defeated and in a few moments, their loved ones would be with the Lord.

Do you wonder how a mother could encourage her young son to confess Christ in the threat of death, and stand by encouraging him, while losing him? Because love wins and she knew He is greater.

Do you ever watch someone whose life has been wrecked and notice greater joy and contentment than someone else whose life, by all appearances, is easy? That person, too, has learned the secret that love triumphs because Christ is greater than the world or anything in it. And in the face of whatever troubles you, you, too, may enter untroubled rest.

Because love wins and joy is a gift!

"Father, thank you that your promises remain steadfast in death and in life."

DAY 55

*"And Jesus answered them, 'Those who are well have no need of a
physician, but those who are sick.*

"'I have not come to call the righteous but sinners to repentance.'"

Luke 5:31–32, ESV

In Genesis 5, the generations of Adam are listed in order.
Kenan lived and died, Mahalelel lived and died, Jared lived
and died.

When Enoch comes along, it doesn't merely say he lived
and died, but mentions that he lived, walked with God, again
that he walked with God, and then, he "... was not, for God
took him" (Genesis 5:24, NKJV).

Repentance is turning from our natural paths to walking
with God. It is common for people to live and die—it is un-
common for someone to walk with God. A few thousand years
later we are still reading the fact that Enoch walked with God.

Repentance is a gift because being a child of God is a gift.
It defines you. It brings you into the greatest love ever named or
experienced by mankind. You belong. You are born again into
something other than the old you.

**You are made new. And you can't be new before you repent
of the old and surrender to the new.**

You get to live for what matters. You get to know your destiny. You get to agree with God about the yuck in you and cast it aside for a better, new you. Many shrink under the promptings of the Spirit to own up to and repent of sin or mistakes because they do not see the gift that it is.

We love when our kids are truly sorry for what they've done. We love to grant them forgiveness and a new beginning. New beginnings are so awesome we quickly forget what they've done. But new beginnings don't happen without penitence and turning away, changing, being made new.

Repentance leads us right to the throne room for unmerited favor. We turn from all we are, to all He is.

When love reaches down to remove your yuck, you get to extend more love to those around you because love reached down and brought you back to His heart, and *His heart always extends the good, the glorious, the beautiful.*

He wants your sin out of the way so your heart can be graced with glory. As you allow Him, you will find your soul bathed in beauty you never knew existed. No matter what you've been, no matter where you've been, He offers beauty to your soul.

Many Christians are more intent on becoming confident and self-aware than they are in being repentant and God-aware. We must acknowledge our own sinfulness before we can accept forgiveness. And we cannot accept forgiveness if we think we are "good" people with no need for a savior each and every day.

Being a Christian has nothing to do with being good—it has everything to do with allowing Goodness to dwell within you.

Daily, I find myself in utter need of redemption. Daily, it's a gift to be received by faith. Daily, a humble posture before the

Lord. From that place, we find confidence in Him and He leads us to peace.

We cannot be truly awed with the Lord without first seeing our own sinfulness. Kneeling at the foot of the cross for unmerited grace and favor allows our hearts to bend low in worship to an awesome God.

Acknowledging our need opens the door for light to wash our souls and worship to fill our hearts.

"There is none righteous, no, not one" (Romans 3:10, NKJV).

Those who hold on to any sense of righteousness other than that given by Christ are losing out on one of the most vital elements of knowing Jesus. He came, not to "call the righteous, but sinners, to repentance." He hung out with sinners so He could grant them mercy, could change their lives.

Repentance is the bedrock on which faith grows best. There is no room for our own righteousness and the Lord's; once we willingly give up our own, He fills us with His. But we must be absolutely done with our own efforts, and yield to His Spirit instead.

When we surrender, He begins. It's that simple. And when He begins, righteousness becomes a fruit flowing from our lives rather than something we muster up each day with draining effort. He is life, but we must be dead in order for Him to live.

"Unless a grain of wheat falls into the ground and dies, it remains alone; but if it dies, it produces much grain" (John 12:24, NKJV).

If you are in that place of saying, "I can't, and I quit," you are in the best place you've ever been. Because God can, when you can't; and He can't, when you still think you can!

Each and every day, begin your day with this posture of heart because this will enable Christ to move right in, stay in, and abide with you.

"Father, help us not to shy away from repentance,
but to see it as the gift it is."

DAY 56

"Then He opened their minds to understand the scriptures, and said to them, 'Thus it is written, that the Christ should suffer and on the third day rise from the dead,

"'And that repentance and forgiveness of sins should be proclaimed in His name to all nations.'" Luke 24:46–47, ESV

Nehemiah mourned over sin even though it was not necessarily his own. Not only did he mourn, he made request to the king and gave his life and energy to remedy what sin had destroyed. When enemies tried to hinder the work, he rallied men to bravery and stood strong for his cause (Nehemiah 1–4).

He didn't only mourn; he worked for positive change. He led, rallied, and stood.

I see true repentance here. A heart of grief leading to change. A heart willing to do what it took to bring about drastic reform. Strong bravery in the face of opposition.

This is the kind of strength we have when God is truly leading us. Something about the Spirit of Christ is invincible and undeniable, and we stand no matter what or who threatens us to fall. Even after a mess-up, we get to stand strong because God redeems and the Spirit intercedes, and the power of life is stronger than death.

When the Spirit intercedes on our behalf, all of heaven's power moves.

When we are truly repentant, we need to accept God's forgiveness and move on. Humility or repentance do not keep hanging on to a feeling of despair or failure. True repentance learns from mistakes and moves forward, resolving, by God's grace, not to relive the past.

Sometimes, especially when our failures hurt others, this is difficult. I have had many such experiences, and it is difficult to accept forgiveness and move on. I want to "fix it," but the fact remains that I am human and need to receive forgiveness just as I want others to accept my forgiveness.

Receiving forgiveness allows me to learn and grow, move past and beyond my mistakes, and become whole in spite of my imperfections.

Receiving forgiveness humbles us to the point of being gracious with the faults of others. We acknowledge that we are in need of forgiveness we don't deserve, and are therefore able to extend the same forgiveness to others. We begin to see others as imperfect human beings, just as we, and are not as surprised or hurt when others fail us. We know we have done the same thing.

Releasing others from a standard of perfection liberates us. This is especially true for our closest loved ones. We are set free to love and continue loving even when they fail or hurt us. We turn the tables and realize they do the same for us. What a liberating truth to acknowledge and put into practice!

Repentant women are quick to forgive because they have already received their own forgiveness at the foot of the cross.

Repentant women are quick to say, "I'm sorry." They acknowledge their needs and readily admit to them.

Repentant women receive correction. In fact, they welcome correction because they know that seeing is not always complete with their own eyes.

Repentant women are the happiest women. They are washed, and extend the same forgiveness to others. Therefore, no bitterness or hidden sins remain to destroy the soul.

"Lord, help us to look to you for perfection as we release others and ourselves to come to you for cleansing."

Day 57

"A scoffer does not like to be reproved; he will not go to the wise."
Proverbs 15:12, ESV

"But Daddy, my other naughty friends are even more naughty."

Our minivan was loaded, and, as is usually the case, instruction was necessary for the four-year-old. He wanted Daddy's approval, but instead needed correction. In one split second, he came up with the solution—make someone else appear worse than he was.

My husband and I eyed each other with a smile in our eyes. Wow! Never expected that one.

And then, of course, my mind raced to adults and how, though they may never voice it so point-blank, their actions and words display an aggressive need to point out the other's fault instead of looking at their own. We hear that rebuke and, bam! Our first instinct is to justify.

"He who hates correction will die" (Proverbs 15:10, NKJV).

We are not responsible for others' sins; we are responsible for our own, and for every bit of our own whether we think it was self-induced or we blame it on another.

It takes genuine humility to own up to our own faults and sins. Human nature demands that others' sins be taken care of first. We reason that once we are no longer wronged, we can repent easily. *This is not how kingdom love operates.*

Kingdom values appear upside down to our own. For us, the way up is the way down.

Doing our own part will free us up, and our freedom is never based on someone else's performance. Never does God ask us to care for our hearts if someone else takes care of his. *He calls us to purity based on His values, not on others' obedience to those values.*

Our calling to righteousness is unshakable. This is why you can never, ever blame your sin on another regardless of how much or little you've been wronged.

If you recall, the Son of Man and Creator of the world said, "Father, forgive them, for they know not what they do" (Luke 23:34, NKJV) even as his own creation was crucifying Him. If anyone had a right to sin and blame it on others, it was Jesus. But He kept His heart pure.

Few things are as healing as hearing someone say, "I'm sorry." Those two simple words, sincerely given, wash away months' or years' worth of hurt. Let's make sure we acknowledge our sin, whether we are most at fault, or least. Nothing will free you up more, or free those you've offended more. You may even bring another to repentance by your own sincere apology. Give it freely, whether you are most at fault or not, and watch God move as a result.

Repentance is a vital part of the Christian life, but sometimes we expect perfection from ourselves or others. We feel threatened and humiliated as soon as we've messed up, and angry at others for doing so.

Others know you've failed whether or not you acknowledge it. You can restore trust and relationships when you readily admit what you've failed in. If you do, they may admit their own as well, but even if they don't, your heart is free and light returns to your soul.

You are guilt free and shame free even if they do not extend forgiveness.

Shame tells you that you are a mistake. Guilt says you made a mistake. Seeing the difference enables us to verbally acknowledge our wrong. Shame results in secrecy, silence, and judgment; guilt brings us to repentance, which results in freedom, life, and love.

Remember, "Godly sorrow produces repentance leading to salvation, *not to be regretted;* but the sorrow of the world produces death" (2 Corinthians 7:10, NKJV).

We confuse the two. We blindly try to explain away our failure because of the shame we feel, but fail to realize that owning our guilt is the first step to freedom.

Godly sorrow is a gift. God's discipline is a favor offered to bring peace.

Shame (worldly sorrow) brings death as you wallow in worthlessness. Repentance allows you to make your wrongs right, and allow Godly sorrow for your sin to wash over you.

Jesus will meet you there at the foot of His cross and lift your burden.

*"Father, help us always to own our need,
then to receive your grace."*

Day 58

"Go through, go through the gates! Prepare the way for the people; build up, build up the highway! Take out the stones; lift up a banner for the peoples.

"Indeed, the Lord has proclaimed to the end of the world: 'Say to the daughter of Zion, "Surely your salvation is coming; behold, His reward is with Him, and His work before Him."

"'And they shall call them The Holy People, the Redeemed of the Lord; and you shall be called Sought Out, A City Not Forsaken.'" Isaiah 62:10, NKJV

You may not be able to alter your circumstances, but God will alter your heart when you put Him above your circumstances.

We are a royal priesthood. Royalty does not bend to degradation. Royalty does not hang its head, does not mope about life as if it's too difficult to bear. Royalty is always royal no matter what happens around it.

So we are, as daughters of the King. So many ladies walk about as anything but royalty. Their very birthright as daughters fades from their hearts and they begin to walk about as if it didn't exist.

Begin to worship, and feel the effect it has on your soul as *you are surprisingly lifted high above the tangible, and watch it give way to the spiritual.*

Worship enables us to serve Him with joy. We delight in Him so much that all other delights become secondary. This is power. Power to give, to sacrifice, to respond in obedience. We have tasted and cannot be without.

When Christ becomes our love, we dare not replace Him with something less, or we would be destroyed by the lesser.

The human soul is created with great capacity. This is why we long, in the depths of our soul, for something greater than we know in ourselves.

We try to fill these longings with many things; perhaps relationships, perhaps success, or even fulfillment in ministering to others. These longings may be satisfied for a while in our own circumstances or relationships, but at the end of the day, *the heart still longs for more than it knows.*

Perhaps you are one of those who feels stripped of all things you desire. Has your child passed away, your spouse been gone for years, your life interrupted with sudden illness? Worship for you can be even richer, because He wants to meet your need with His grace.

Remember, He calls it "the sacrifice of praise" (Jeremiah 33:11). This is when you don't want to praise, but you do anyway. *He loves to come with power in those moments.*

It is then you will discover that the love and delight found in worship to Him transcends everything you could feel on this earth. He is ultimate delight and the greatest feast our souls could partake of.

This, then, is God's invitation for our hearts to be satisfied.

As John Piper says, *"God is most glorified when we are most delighted in Him."*

God wants to share things with you just so you have communion, and just so He can commune with you. He delights in you and wants your company, your friendship.

He loves to be loved, He loves to love you, and He delights to commune with you.

"Lord, thank you that in our humanness, you are pleased to dwell with us and be loved by us."

DAY 59

"[Job was] blameless and upright, one who feared God and shunned evil." Job 1:1, NKJV

One day, a messenger came to tell him that his oxen and donkeys were taken, and his servants struck with the edge of the sword.

Another servant ran to convey the news that fire had consumed his sheep and servants; yet another informed him that his camels were raided and his servants destroyed.

The last, most dreadful news was that all his children were killed while they were dining together in their oldest brother's house.

One of these tragedies is enough to shake the faith of most people. Consider how Job, who was blameless and upright, one whom God would boast about when Satan came and stood before him, responded:

"Then Job arose, tore his robe, and shaved his head; and he fell to the ground and worshiped. And he said, 'Naked I came from my mother's womb and naked I shall return there. The Lord gave, and the Lord has taken away. Blessed be the name of the Lord" (Job 1:20–21, NKJV).

This story is the epitome of true worship. Would that all our hearts were in that place. *The glory of God is not diminished by our own trials; He stands, has stood, and will forever stand to be gloriously exalted.*

If Job had chosen to "Curse God and die" (Job 2:9, NKJV) as his wife told him he should, the trials Satan had brought to accomplish that very purpose would have been realized.

Job had no idea he was on trial for the triumph of God. He was simply faithful, saying, "But He knows the way that I take; when He has tested me, I shall come forth as gold" (Job 23:10, NKJV).

When your heart is burning in worship, any grief, pain, trial, or loss you may feel is fuel for the fire of worship. Fire falls on sacrifice. You sacrifice much to worship through, and in spite of, these things.

When we worship for the return we want, it can easily turn into manipulation. When we worship Him simply because we choose Him to be all, this is true worship.

Problems do not define God; solutions do. When we worship anyway, God goes out and fights for us. He returns from war and calls us mighty warriors, when all we did was praise and worship Him.

Even in doubt, you can never go wrong when you worship.

When you are confused as to the path you should take, worship Him for promising to give wisdom, then promising grace and peace to carry out that wisdom. *You are never, ever lost when you are enthralled with Christ.* Grace that you didn't feel will come, courage you lack entirely will enter your soul.

When a person bows low before the Lord, He lifts them up.

There is no greater power to do right than to have God Himself enter your soul. He always brings us low so He can be high, then *He chooses to lift our hearts so high we stand entirely amazed.*

"Father, help us to worship you in all things."

DAY 60

"Abide in Me, and I in you. As the branch cannot bear fruit of itself unless it abide in the vine, neither can you, unless you abide in Me."
John 15:4, ESV

Her eyes snapped and sparkled, and I thought, "I want to be like her when I'm older." She had vibrancy, and it didn't come from just anywhere.

Not everyone works for a company profiting $48,000,000,000 in one quarter. She worked from home, at that.

Logging in to her computer is a regular occurrence, but she spoke more of logging in to the Lord each morning. Her job was important, but Christ moreso. And as she traveled and worked and lived, she kept having God encounters with others — because she was *logged in.*

We may not have time or energy to rise early every morning. I don't always get to watch the sun rise over the bay in a yellow glow because truth is, I'm too exhausted. Some nights are late and schedules aren't perfect.

But worship is a state of being more than doing.

I woke this morning with the sun shedding glimmers of light just at the crack of dawn, and it hit me, this whole, brand-new day fresh and open before me. I could only say, "God, it's yours."

Psalm 100:4–5 speaks of entering His gates with thanksgiving. Somehow, we must enter each day. Giving back to God what is His to begin with is a form of worship. We draw near, we ask what He is doing more than tell Him what we want to do.

Not because we have to, but when our hearts are in awe of Him, *we want to.*

We're not just living life and going places for ourselves. When we're logged in, we change atmospheres because we emit kingdom life to those around us. **God's grace becomes a beacon emitting rays of light, drawing others, bypassing the natural right into the spiritual.**

Safe water has both an in and an out source of flow. Whether your time is thirty seconds or an entire hour, make sure you have an inflow of light, and that you give the light you have all the place it needs to shine.

Christ comes into your heart, and His love goes out of your life to those around you. But He must come in before His love can go out.

Ask God what He's thinking. It may be, as you live this way, you will begin touching lives like my friend Lora does, whether they are strangers in the airport or friends from her hometown. You may have words to share or be led to impromptu acts of kindness to strangers you will never see again.

Because knowing Jesus is so much more than a focus on living right; knowing Jesus looks more like sharing light just like He did. We cannot be both stagnant and alive.

Posture yourself; log in; enter His gates, each and every day.

"Lord, help us to log into you as we begin each day."

DAY 61

"Let the heavens be glad, and let the earth rejoice, and let them say among the nations, 'The Lord reigns!'" 1 Chronicles 16:31, ESV

I stared into his eyes, which still glowed with life, despite the way age and sickness had taken its toll on his body.

He began to speak, words that come only from the heart undone, *the soul looking up with nowhere else to go.* I listened in silence, eyes riveted. There was so much here, straight from the mouth of a man who was told he would meet his maker soon.

The worship we'll know in heaven, he said, will be as grand in comparison to earthly tones as lovely music is to fingernails scratching on a chalkboard. I stood, fascinated, soaking it in. It's a rare privilege to listen to a soul set on worship, God, and all that really matters.

He was enchanted with heaven because heaven had already come to his heart. For him, eternity began many years ago.

He was more concerned about his dear wife than he was about getting well. More intent on phone calls and numbers on paper assuring him that she would be cared for. He was more focused on peace and worship than he was upset about the threat of death.

He was ready to go, because his heart had already grasped the power, long ago. "What's the worst thing that could happen to me?" he asked, eyes looking at mine for an answer.

I didn't want to say it, but I did, softly. "Dying."

"Exactly." His voice strained to speak because the evil cancer had already attacked his body to stage four. "And it's not all that bad."

I could only smile weakly and nod in agreement. I loved these people, and when you love, you weep when they weep, smile when they rejoice, and sometimes you know that brave smiles are an aftermath of salty tears spilled in the night.

They served me lunch, this dear couple intent on finding God in the shattering of their golden years.

We held each other and prayed to the God who gives and takes away, who heals our souls as well as our bodies whether it be here, or there.

For many years he had prayed for heaven to come to earth. Now, as he prepares for earth to come to heaven, for mortality to be dissolved in immortal life, he continues to worship.

More hugs, more whispered words of love, and I left the little green house in a holy hush. He knew what life was all about; that if faith is worth living for, it is also strong enough to carry us right into death, and beyond.

Worship begins here, now, today. Let heaven come to earth in your heart, and mine. *In this way, we are prepared to live fully, and death is but a door to an even fuller life.*

A few hours before, I met new life in the face of a newborn. One cannot help but gaze steadily into the eyes of a child so small, such a masterpiece of heaven. Her little brothers tumbled about, and Mama tried to keep them steady in the course of the day.

She was a picture of heaven here. I compared the two faces, one so small, fresh, and new; the other, worn and tired but with new life written on his face.

I'd say heaven has come to earth, in both; life was displayed in both. For the one, a new beginning here; for the other, splashes of hope for a new beginning, there.

God is all about new beginnings. He moves, He works, He touches each life with a stroke of His brush, and all of it is beautiful. Finding Him in your own moment will be your heaven come, your eternity begun, your soul united, your moment leading you straight ahead to all that is.

In an odd, breathtaking way, heaven coming down to bring a soul to the bosom of the Father is even more beautiful than a newborn baby beginning life on this earth.

So rise on, soul. Soar up and ahead. May heaven and earth meet in your heart and mine, wherever we are, today.

"Lord, thank you that eternity begins here, now, today; that when we die we are merely continuing on with what has already been given us."

DAY 62

"The hour is coming, when you will neither on this mountain, nor in Jerusalem, worship the Father. . . . But true worshipers will worship the Father in spirit and in truth; for the Father is seeking such to worship Him." John 4:21–23, NKJV

I stared at the waves one day, my eyes locked on to beauty I had no words for.

I saw it.

God is in the waves. He is seen in fire. He is heard in the wind. Have you ever felt the soul inside of you squirm because you had no words, could not place the glory you saw, felt too small and incomplete beside such grandeur?

I have. But today it was as if I saw Him in those waves. That rushing wall of blue power rolling toward the heavens spoke but one thing to me: God.

I think that's why He made beauty too lovely for me to soak in. He really wants me to see Him in it, because when He's in me fully, all else fades and I see Him, worship Him, know Him.

He's the pearl of great price.

Pearls are formed by the rubbing of one thing against another. In Revelation, the gate is made of pearls. *So in our lives, irritations can be the gateway to seeing beauty.*

When all is perfect in our lives, we do not long for deliverance. When all is pain free, we need no healing. If all was lovely, the magnificent would not stand in stark contrast.

Worship calls us to the heart of God in all we do. *The shout of victory that permeates the core of Christianity is this all-inclusive, non-exclusive triumph of the soul declaring love to be the winner.*

We feel God in the wind, see Him in the waves, follow hard after Him in the irritations of life while He turns ugly things into pearls. When we know someone as big as God, we make much of Him. He's more than a nice idea floating around the universe—He's the master potter behind the wheel—and He knows what He's doing!

Worship does not begin or end Sunday mornings or during your quiet time. Worship is the posture of your heart before the Lord more than it is a time or service.

Because God is Spirit, and because His Spirit dwells with the lowly and contrite, the very presence of Himself in our hearts means we are in a state of worship. When we are so full that we see Him, feel Him, know Him, are more delighted in Him than anything else—this is worship.

Ladies, this is the place our Father calls us to. When you rise in the morning and your thoughts turn to the Lord in delight, when you are grateful that you get to have Him with you all day, when you know that you know Him and no matter what happens that day, He will still be your joy; this is worship.

Worship is not confined to a stage or place; true worship is lived out daily.

"Lord, thank you that hard places form the best kind of pearls. Help us believe you for that, today. Change us into pearls."

Day 63

"In all your ways acknowledge Him, and He will make straight your paths." Proverbs 3:6, ESV

I stared at the bridge spanning ahead of me, curving round, daring to defy the depths of air and trees beneath. It held my kids. Our kids.

They walked safely to the other side, but one nearly didn't. As my eyes averted only a few seconds, he climbed up, up, and up on the rail meant to hold him in. He stood, leaning toward scary depths while his feet barely held to the rail.

I screamed, and reached to pull him down. "Mama, I was only this high." He pointed to a board lower than the one he had actually been on, and I quickly let him know that he was higher, and that it was not safe. Not OK.

We walked on, and I thought about how bridges come to be. Someone comes to a precipice and there is no way around, no way through, no way under—unless they build a bridge. The daring soul who wills his desire into reality begins the project. Others follow suit, and sooner or later, the gulf is spanned.

That scary precipice in your life . . . what is it? Most likely, it will not go away, but needs to be conquered, somehow. You may stand there the rest of your life wishing it away, you may cry that it's there in the first place, you may reach for things to help you cope with its presence. But soul, scared-out-of-your-wits soul, angry soul, hurting soul, how will you span the gulf and come to the other side?

When there's no way under, no way around, no way above, then, well, you take a deep breath and you walk right through. You hang on to truth tenaciously, blind your eyes to the scary depths, and you walk. You keep walking.

The precipice God asks you to walk over won't be easy—but it will be *best*.

When you stop, as did my son, and reach into the air for answers that aren't there, you will fall. There is nothing but the word God speaks right under your feet. And He says to you, there is a way through, right through, straight through the precipice if you dare Him to bring you there.

He will pull you down from the rail if you lean into the precipice searching for answers when the bridge He's built for you is already under your feet, willing you to keep walking.

The bridge we walked on that day was long. It curved to the right, luring us around the corner to safe ground. Small cubicles on the side reminded us that once, trains came speeding across the gulf and would, perhaps, need water to quench some angry flame that dared burst forth even while the life of everyone depended on the bridge.

Danger and risk accompanied each soul who chose to trust there was a way across and through the span of air and treetops. But right along with the risk were large containers of water for supply. Just in case.

We walked safely across that day. And with each precipice in our lives, we may trust there is a bridge to bring us through to a better side, and there are provisions for the heart along the way. He is a good Father, and He shows us His goodness right in the center of those bridges, where we walk safely above the abyss.

We have only to trust His word, just as we trusted those boards beneath us not to give way.

We have only to follow Him around the curve when we can't see the end, just as my kids trustingly turned that bend, knowing it would take them one step closer to town for the treat they wanted.

Because following God's sure word always brings us one step closer to His heart and His desired end for us.

"Father, help us follow your sure words to us,
whether they lead us over a precipice or through a valley. Help
us trust what we know is true, that you always
bring us safely to the other side."

DAY 64

"He is not afraid of bad news; his heart is firm, trusting in the Lord."
Psalm 112:7, ESV

It was 9/11, that day when countenances sober and tears still fall for many people. In others, fear rises because, what if it happens again?

My own brother died in the deep waters of a lake in South America. My mind shuts down when I try to imagine what he must have felt. But how much more the family members of those in the towers who hurled themselves out windows and died a crushing death on streets below?

I'm sure thoughts of their loved ones fearing the fire enveloping them makes them want to go crazy. Who would want to see such terror written on a loved one's face, to know the decision they faced to die in flames, or hurl themselves to an instant death hundreds of feet below?

As smoke billowed from the towers, bystanders were in shock. As the towers fell, even greater disbelief. And as rescuers searched heaps of rubbish for people yet alive, the tragedy continued.

It really never ended. Those memories won't just leave, though we wish they could.

It's difficult to imagine a soul wicked enough to cause such terror purposefully. Or be deceived enough to think their god wants them to do so. Or be willing enough to die themselves to accomplish all of it. Most soldiers fight to live, not die. What must have taken over their minds to cause them to do such damage?

Really, what takes over any of our minds when we hurt each other?

Evil men will always be here, and they will always do their thing. Those around you will always be human and will do their thing, too. And you, though you may want to think otherwise, are also human and have full capability of bringing hurt to those you love.

Codependency means you aren't able to be at peace unless others do right. Or even unless others do what you think you need them to do for your happiness and well-being. You are always looking, searching, longing for life apart from yourself.

You need others to fill a vacancy in your heart, and if they don't, you break.

When evil men do their thing, you seethe with bitterness or fall apart in despair.

When your friends or family mess up and cause you grief, you can't rest until they are set straight.

You forget that if you focus so much on their sin, you become absorbed by it until you are no longer healthy, either.

You forget that you don't wrestle against flesh and blood, but against principalities and powers who are out to destroy you, and they often do it through other people.

You spin crazy, you go nuts, you say you've had too much and can't handle life anymore. All because you're allowing the darts to penetrate rather than wielding them away with your own strength given you by God, because He's your Father.

None of us are dependent on another for our happiness.

But aren't we designed to need others, to live life with those who love us and fill certain needs?

Yes, but they are a gift. We were never meant to go down because another is down. Never meant to grasp for happiness, but rather to receive the free gift of joy.

Strength and joy are yours to receive whether evil men do their thing or not. Those family members of martyrs killed by ISIS knew this truth, which is why they sat there with peace and forgiveness, testifying to the world of their desire to see salvation come to the killers.

Yes, they sorrowed; yes, it was more difficult than anything they had ever experienced. *But they were not destroyed.*

Bitter people have yet to accept the free gift. Bitter people haven't yet discovered that they can mourn, but still live; they can hurt, but still find healing; they may sorrow, but still live in grace. *They haven't yet learned that life doesn't hang on the balance of another fallible human being.*

The presence of God must be stronger than the presence of wrong. He's already won the powers of darkness; allow Him to win the posture of your heart, and you will find yourself with His life even when those same powers wreak havoc to your circumstances.

Nothing can destroy Him, so nothing can destroy you.

Is He greater to you than others are? Can you walk in peace even if you suffer their lack, their humanness? 1 John 4:4 says, "Greater is He who is in me than He who is in the world."

He's given you power, love, and a sound mind because that's Who He is (2 Timothy 1:7).

The victims of 9/11 never suffered the aftermath their loved ones have. And each of those family members must choose whether or not to be victimized into bitterness, or to realize they are greater than even these powers of darkness.

And we, in our own small or great ways, must leave dependency behind and reach for our very own life, all because it's free.

"Father, thank you that we are not dependent on anyone but you for inner strength and life."

DAY 65

"He only is my rock and my salvation; he is my defense; I shall not be greatly moved." Psalms 62:2, NKJV

"I did it!"

His blue eyes sparkled as he turned his head to make sure I was watching. He still had training wheels on the bike, to be sure, but he felt that gliding, smooth feel as he balanced alone for a few split seconds.

I cheered for him, while my heart beat every bit as happy as his.

We reached the curve, and he paused, willing the little green bike to make the turn without a fall. I let go of my grip and watched. He started crying. "Mama, you can't let go!"

He made the turn safely and stopped cold, right in the center of the road. "Mama, you really can't let go! I like your hands here, right here." And he touched both sides of his waist, the most secure spot for steadying hands.

I agreed, and next time I held my hands out, around, that chubby little tummy. Barely touching, gently letting him know I was there without helping along. He thought I held him, and rounded the turn smoothly before joyfully gliding ahead. He was thrilled.

Mama "helped," but she didn't really help. All he needed was faith that he could, and he did. He trusted that Mama was right there, that Mama wouldn't let him fall flat. Trusted that his knees wouldn't scrape hard on pavement, that he wouldn't get hurt. Trusted that everything would be fine.

He had strength, then. Strength of heart, which allowed him to steer smoothly, safely, happily, with confidence. It was awesome to watch. I touched him lightly, but he did the thing I was wanting him to do. All because he trusted my touch.

I remembered my own shivering, cold self in the pool the other day, trying to get over this lifelong water paranoia. Thinking of putting my head underwater simply drove me into a panic while I stood there, frustrated, watching tiny kids dive and spin and twirl in the water.

Up they came, faces alight with thrill. And there I stood, downcast with fear.

This summer I decided this was it. I was learning to swim. I couldn't do it unless someone strong and big and tall was right there. He led me out, this friend of ours who taught many others, way out to water above my shoulders and up my neck while I gave every ounce of strength I could muster to follow him. He held my hands while I shook with cold and panic, but we went out, and out, and out. My toes barely touched the bottom of the pool, and I clung as tightly as I could. I had to do this, no matter what, or I would always be held in this vise, this grip that clung to me even when it was silly to be afraid.

I walked on. I could go, because someone was there.

It got a little easier that day.

Next time, there I stood again, willing myself to try, miserable with cold and gripped in fear. My husband took my hands and I dunked. It wasn't so bad. I hung on tightly and let my legs float in the water where he stood, close. The feel of it all thrilled me, this letting go of fear and trusting my body to the water.

Thoughts of my brother's body in water, of him going down and down never to surface again alive, came at me, chilled my brain colder than the water washing my skin. I pushed the thoughts aside, shoved them away so I could do this. I hung on tightly and kept trying as it became easier and easier. Soon I was letting go, moving a little, then halfway across the pool. He stood there, tall and strong, ready to catch me if I needed him.

He didn't laugh at my fear of water—he just led me, caught me, stood there as I pulled at him hard when a wave of fear washed over me.

As long as he was there, I could do it. As long as he stayed there, I could turn away gripping thoughts of my brother, and trust anyway. As long as he stood, tall and strong, always close, that accumulation of paranoia had to give way to the presence of strength and safety close by.

I realized he was a picture of Christ to me. When I am confident that Christ has me, that it is He who leads me, He who is speaking, I need nothing more. **When God speaks, you just can't argue.** When He leads, you can follow without fear because His end always holds greater blessing than our own. Other things must and do give way when we follow. Even our feelings may change as God wraps Himself into the fiber of our beings with His good word to us.

If we don't follow, our feelings may never change, and we will be stuck in a life of our own making. God's word is perfection, and He leads us on to better things, washes our own thoughts, and changes fear into strength. I would never know the thrill of water if I didn't hang on and will myself to let go of my own thoughts because I trusted something greater than my feelings.

It's just that we need to know, really know, God is there. To feel His steadying hands around us as we want to turn left or right. *If He is leading, we may rest assured, and if He is speaking, we may turn all other voices silent in recognition of, and submission to, the greater One.*

Find His touch and fall into it, lean into it, rest well in it. You will always come out right when you lean hard, trust hard, and follow hard. He has you, and it is here you are safe. He holds you, and it is here you are stronger than strength itself, because He is.

Women of strength let go of their own, for strength not their own.

> "Lord, thank you that when we hold on to you,
> we find the strength we've been looking for."

DAY 66

"Those who trust in the Lord are like Mt. Zion, which cannot be moved, but abides forever. As the mountains surround Jerusalem, so the Lord surrounds His people." Psalm 125:1–2, ESV

We pulled on the heavy packs, my man and I, and gazed into the endless green mountains. Today we were going up, up, and up some more.

Our friends led the way, and the path was steep. I watched her feet, and followed the leader through rocks, streams, up steep inclines, and down slippery slopes. My husband's knee throbbed, my heart pounded, while others were drenched in sweat with hours more of winding trail going *up*.

I couldn't go on; but I could. All I had to do was watch her feet and follow. The kind guide offered to pause. We didn't need to look back or forward, but weigh our attention fully to the next step, no matter how difficult.

My husband, my own strong, kind man, offered to take my pack when he was already loaded with his and had a throbbing knee. I shook my head, bent my back, and kept climbing. But his offer refreshed the heart and I knew I was walking with the right people.

We finally reached one of the most magnificent places on the planet.

Jagged peaks jutted into the vast blue, and the lake shone turquoise in the sunlight. Patches of snow were surrounded with wildflowers, and fish leaped wildly into the air before plunging into the deep waters.

All was still, and all was well. More than well—it was magnificence defined.

Here, where the heart goes silent except in its quest to the Creator. Here, where all is as it should be, God speaks to my soul in ways I can't hear when I'm rushing about with life on the street. Here where mountains tower high and flowers bloom in colors so vibrant it takes my breath away. Where you wake in the morning to wild nature, calm in its original state, and the heart wonders where it's been. Here, where you see a bird, pause, and ask to be like it, just like it.

But it was hard work to get here. And I needed others with me.

Our leader slowed his pace for us ladies; he didn't push ahead, but waited so we could walk together.

A friend offered me her walking stick when the trail got steep.

My strong husband brought up the rear so he could watch for any danger and keep us safe.

We paused to eat along the way.

Wildflowers cheered us as they bloomed in sunny meadows before the path rose steep again.

The trail wasn't endless, and led us straight to beauty and rest.

Friends, what are you working hard to get to?

Make sure you are following the right leader; God never walks faster than you are able.

Walk with friends who will help you along. *Walking alone is not an option if you want to get there safely.*

If you are afraid, have someone behind you to watch out for danger. Don't be embarrassed that you need it; *we are not meant to walk the trail alone while others stand on the side observing how well we do.*

Pause for refreshments—time alone, time spent doing what you love, time to hear the Lord and find His strength. He's provided refreshments and we have only to receive them.

Remember the path won't always stay steep. Look forward to wildflowers and sunny meadows.

Remember that all trials do end, and if you follow the right leader, He will doubtless lead you into beauty and rest.

Remember this most of all: Walking alone is not an option. Follow your good, wise Leader, and join others who are walking the same trail. Accept their walking sticks, and offer them yours. If you fall behind, reach for an arm to pull you forward, and always keep an eye out for those who need yours. Never leave another in the dust. Thank the guy bringing safety to the group, and don't begin unless he's there. And last but not least, thank the leader for navigating the trail and setting a pace that pushed you, but didn't destroy you.

"Father, thank you that you've given us others to walk with, and You are our Leader who will never lead too fast or far."

DAY 67

"Do you not know that in a race all the runners run, but only one receives the prize? So run that you may obtain it." 1 Corinthians 9:24, ESV

I close the bedroom door softly, the door that barely shuts out the noise of four kids from my husband sleeping after a night at work. He needs sleep after having to let a girl know her daddy has just been killed, after taking a drunk to jail, and after working sixteen hours.

I step into the old running shoes that have run many a mile for not one, but two, women. They're a bit bent and certainly not pretty, but they do the trick.

My heart pounds this early in the morning, but I get to smell fresh air laden with honeysuckle, get to see the world before it's buzzing with cars and people, get to watch fog lift over the bay where the beach is sodden with tide far removed from its shore.

The world is still, beautiful, fresh. I get to experience it because I'm choosing to leave my comfortable bed, and run.

My mind takes wing to those things that hinder me, us. The things that weigh us down, the things we really need to move beyond so we can experience the next good thing the Lord wants to do in our hearts.

I realize I need to run. Run with what God is saying. Run so hard with it that I'm led right into beauty and rest of heart.

I can't stay in the comfort zone of muddling my own way through. Can't stay one more day, or I'll miss out, a whole lot. I won't ever know the fulfillment of God's promises over my life if I never run with them, and run away from the rest.

Those nagging troubles of the heart can be left behind, and we may go hard after more, better, good. Either we pursue the good, or we are overcome by the bad—and the bad is only as powerful as we allow it to be.

Runners for the Olympics train brutally, beat their bodies into hard-core strength. It hurts; it takes willpower, everything they can muster. They would never win if they stayed in their pajamas eating pancakes.

In our walks with God, Paul urges us to "run, that we may obtain." He says they run to receive an earthly prize, but we, a heavenly one. Our training is to trust and rest and follow— theirs is to push and sweat and move.

Today, dare run hard after a solid promise from your Father who cannot lie to you, and never will.

Dare leave the comfort zone of your own thoughts, and break out into a hard, fast run after His own.

Dare watch one beautiful thing after another unfold in your soul.

When The Lord led the people of Israel out of Egypt, He sent an angel before them to bring them to the Amorites, Hittites, Perizzites, and other tribes. He promised to blot them out by sending hornets before them, and to bless His people if they held to His ways and didn't bow to other gods when life became easy after they conquered the land.

But what else did the Lord say? He said He "would not

drive them out before you in one year . . . but little by little . . ." (Exodus 23:29–30 NKJV). He would drive them out until they possessed the land.

I paused and considered. You know how we all want and subconsciously expect the Lord to wipe our problems away the instant we pray? We know He's stronger than strength itself and we depend on Him to lighten our load.

But guess what He may do instead? Allow parts of our trial to stand so the land of our heart doesn't become barren. *He improves our strength by allowing things we need to be strong for.*

It's a little like my friend who started running. She ran hard, sweat rolling down her cheeks, breathing fast. Getting to the marathon was no easy feat, but she did it. And it was worth every bit of effort.

So it is with acquiring strength in the Lord.

Eternity begins in our hearts here, now, today as we are stripped of our own strength, and sink into His.

*"Lord, thank you that you never push us for no reason.
Thank you that there are always rich dividends
when we push hard after you."*

DAY 68

"But He answered, 'It is written, man shall not live by bread alone, but by every word that comes from the mouth of God." Matthew 4:4, ESV

Her soul was hungry, had been for days; she was empty, and had been for days. But today, she took that leather-bound book of all books to the backyard and sat down at the ancient, weathered picnic table.

Life with four on the run made for short quiet moments, but her eyes feasted. And as they did, she knew. This was what she was missing. She hadn't taken the time to be still, to feast, to feed her soul. Words of life bring life, and her heart swelled and came alive.

It's odd how hungry she felt for life, when the past days were so full of material blessing and fun. But it wasn't enough.

It never is.

If we don't take time to feed our souls like we feed our bodies, we will soon be unable to give life to those around us, just as we would be unable to feed our families if we didn't also feed ourselves.

The body gives out. Our souls give out, too, unless they are fed.

But we're mortal beings with a great propensity for the finite and earthly. We forget about our souls and their place in the kingdom when we forget to enrich them. We rush about and run about, all the while wondering why we're not more satisfied.

I remember the night I got to watch an arrest of a tiny little lady, rendered nearly immobile from the amount of drugs intoxicating her body. The stark contrast between her and the officers struck me forever.

One was creating the mess, immobile in her self-created disaster; the others, active even in the dead of night to bring safety to the world. One, adding to chaos; the others, serving their people and adding life. How in the world do they handle the mess with so much grace, when others line the halls of jail making the mess? How can they be so active in the dead of night while others can only be led in handcuffs, removed from the world so as to remove risk and danger?

Both parties live in a messy world. Both parties make choices, daily. And you must know that some of the men in uniform had the same trials and pains thrown their way as some of the people lining the hallway that night.

As I drove home the moon shone a silent, golden path on the bay. And I knew, as surely as there was a gleam of light in the darkness of night, that each of us is born to shine. Rising above doesn't come easy, friends, but it becomes a personal choice each of us must make. Will we stay in our mess, immobile, causing unrest in our environments? Or will we, like those men in uniform, become strong life-givers because that is our birthright as daughters of the King, regardless of the mess around us?

God is no respecter of persons; He offers life to each soul He created whether or not their world is messed up. Satan also is no respecter of persons, and he brings low all those who stay immobile in the mess of their lives, taking them lower than they ever thought they would go when they listen to lies rather than truth.

Purpose is all about changing what we respond to, all about giving truth the highest place in our lives rather than hurts and lies. It's all about becoming a life-giver and bringing joy to our surroundings because we've found truth to overcome every obstacle.

The choice may be personal, but it is far reaching.

"Lord, thank you that regardless of how old or young we are, it is never too late to begin bringing life to the world."

DAY 69

"Now Amalek came and fought with Israel. . . . When Moses held up his hand, Israel prevailed; and when he let down his hand, Amalek prevailed. But Moses' hands became heavy." Exodus 17:8–12, NKJV

"Mom, she's acting *so silly*!"

One child shakes his head while the other does indeed bob the waves of whatever is bumping around inside her. It is truly annoying, this silly toss-up of emotions making her act like a baby one minute and a goofy monster the next. It does call for some scathing remarks, the other children think, and they dish it out while rolling their eyes in disgust and calling "Earth to Mama!" in hopes that it will jolt me out of the peaceful inner moment I'm enjoying while I ignore the ruckus.

So life continues. Four children get highly annoyed at each other. One child slurps his soup, another nitpicks her way through life, and still another wants to be babied even though she's eight years old—which makes the oldest, levelheaded child croak with distress.

"Mom, she's so annoying!"

And then you enter adult world. One lady coldly passes by another at church because "something happened between us."

The next minute the same lady is chatting happily with some-one else, who apparently hasn't yet crossed her.

I wonder if she knows that the lady she had difficulty with is probably the one who needs her most? I wonder if she looks inside to learn what makes her difficult to relate to, or if she will pass her by the rest of their years together? It's easier to avoid her and not get hurt again, and not be plagued with a relationship that takes genuine effort.

You would think the same God who was causing Israel to win would also strengthen Moses' hands. Why would a mir-acle working God who was already causing the supernatural to happen need two men holding Moses' hands? Because God wants us to work together.

They rallied around him. They set a rock under him for a seat, and held his hands until the sun went down. Moses, the mighty man of God who worked miracles all the time, and was currently right in the center of one, needed help. God wanted his hands up, but he couldn't do it alone. *And his friends, rath-er than scold him for his lack, lifted his hands for him.*

I sat the kids down for worship and prayer time before school this morning, and brought up this mercy thing. "You know, kids, when you get so annoyed with Mama or Daddy or each other, and someone is cranky, it's so easy to roll our eyes and scold whoever is acting out of line. What if, instead, we try to uncover what the real issue is, and help out with the real problem?"

As Alexander Pope says, "To err is human; to forgive, di-vine." What if, instead of being upset that someone is grouchy, we realize they must be having a difficult day and try to help?"

I could see it click with the kids. You know, they all like to be treated that way, but it's so hard to do it with each other in the heat of annoyance. I loved watching this Moses story settle in their hearts and bring about a deeper "knowing" of love, and how to be Jesus to people.

We can minister to others instead of hurt them more. We can dispel the frustration of the day instead of make it worse. We can see hearts soften, lives change, and relationships heal. We can really be Jesus' hands and feet because He said that peacemakers are blessed and they will inherit the kingdom of God.

What if, on the streets, in the church, at home, in the grocery store, we all lived this way? What if?

Puritan Governor John Winthrop was elected twelve times and praised for his liberality, wisdom, piety, generosity, and gravity. To the Puritans, stealing was considered almost as sinful as murder and sometimes resulted in death. During a long, cold winter in Massachusetts, a man was caught stealing wood from Governor Winthrop's yard. When the fact was made known to Governor Winthrop, he promised to put an end to it.

To the thief, he said, "I think you may not have enough wood for the winter. Help yourself to mine whenever you need." And to the man who reported the theft, he said, "I told you I would put an end to it. Now find him stealing again!"

"Father, help us to bring change through love and mercy."

DAY 70

"For I was hungry, and you gave me no food; I was thirsty, and you gave me no drink; I was a stranger, and you did not take me in; naked, and you did not clothe me, sick and in prison and you did not visit me." Matthew 25:42–43, NKJV

"Inasmuch as you did it to one of the least of these my brethren, you did it to me." Matthew 25:40, NKJV

One boy, covered in dust, hungry and afraid; another boy, wealthy and cared for on the other side of the barbed wire.

I hate what the Nazis did to the Jews. I hate the gas chambers and furnaces pouring black smoke with an even blacker stench of burning human flesh. I picture my own little boy starving and my mother's heart wants to go crazy.

I held the kids in my arms tonight after watching "Boy with the Striped Pajamas." We know there are people suffering like that, or worse, today, while we head off to comfy pillows and wake up to more than enough food.

I remind the children to live by what Jesus says, not only by what we see. We don't see these people, but we know they are there. It is so easy for American Christians to forget, to expect the world to pass by the suffering. But God's people? May it not be so!

We tend to measure ourselves with the world's standard of living, forgetting that Christ asks us to be content with food and raiment. We teach our girls (by our own example) that shopping is more fun than giving to those who don't have. We "need" another coat while a mother sits holding her starving baby and there is no milk.

Where is our focus? We think we could do little, but in reality, if our sights were set on the eternal, together we could do a lot. I've been told that if all the wealth in the world was distributed, no one would be hungry. That is the kind of world I want to live in.

I have friends who raise their voices for the abused. I have sisters who travel abroad to bring aid to the suffering. There is no way I am exempt from God's call to mercy and compassion just because I'm a stay-at-home mother of four children who need me. What does God want me to do? How can I raise my voice? How can I sacrifice and give? How can I teach our kids to care, to do, to dare for others?

God calls us to arms in a sick and broken world. We are meant to be caregivers, healers, nurturers. We are called to so much more than decorating our homes and making sure our kids are well taught. There's a hurting world out there, sometimes at our door, and we are called to give.

Giving out means God gives more in to your heart—because He's all about giving.

Giving when it's not easy is so much better than lounging in ease and discovering that in the long run, we're not fulfilled and happy anyway. Allow yourself to cringe with sacrifice for others—*your joy cup will be fuller than if you chose the easy route.*

I know parents who show their kids sacrifice by example. Each Christmas when it's time to buy and wrap gifts, they do so carefully. Then they sit with their kids and choose gifts for the poor while explaining to them this is why they don't splurge more on ourselves. Each year they light up with joy at the thought of a hungry family receiving a goat, chickens, or whatever they choose to give.

Let's be of those who look for opportunity to give, rather than wait until we are asked, then hesitate. Let's watch for giving opportunities as much or more than we watch for great deals or blessings for ourselves. It's a heart thing, a shift in focus, a place where mercy seats itself in the soul and abides there.

"It is more blessed to give than to receive" (Acts 20:35, NKJV).

We can make food for the church's food-for-the-homeless program. Your children will learn to give time and energy by caring for those they don't know.

We can help our kids sell lemonade on a hot day and give the proceeds to refugees.

We can invite those who need friends to our homes.

We can buy a meal for the homeless man on the corner.

We can send extra gifts to sponsored children.

The list is endless. A woman with this heart will succeed in reaching outside the walls of her own home. And she will discover that, as she gives her life, she truly finds it.

"Lord, you ask us to walk as you walked. Help us not be afraid of giving more than we are comfortable with."

DAY 71

"Come to Me, all who labor and are heavy laden, and I will give you rest." Matthew 11:28, NKJV

That moment when mercy wraps you in its arms and holds you close. You've done nothing to deserve it; in fact, done lots of things not to deserve it. But there it is, again.

And the Lord whispers, "I have this. I have you. You can relax your heart, let go of your worry, no matter what it is. Because I am here."

Mercy becomes sweet all over again. Who am I to deserve this? Why would such a perfect God give so much incredible grace to one so full of weakness? Be so patient when I can barely be patient with myself?

But He holds me, right here. Tension drains from my shoulders as I drop the weight of it all. My heart is held, as it were, in softest hands. He has me. He has all that concerns me. And because of this, everything is all right.

The brain running in a hundred different directions to solve fifty different problems suddenly pauses. I am relieved when I realize I can pause the rapid thoughts of my mind, and it's OK not to come up with a solution for life's problems. Just because He has me, and He holds me.

I guess this is why those who receive mercy find themselves with solutions they didn't work for, but received. Mercy is incredibly sweet. Such powerful grace cannot help but work life changes in the heart, which in turn affect all those around you.

Then, I see them, standing beside the road strumming guitars, signs propped up with needs penned out for the world to see. I drive by, and I squirm.

I want to get to know these people, really know them and be their friend. But I drive by because I hear they often spend cash on cigarettes and drugs more than food. Someone even told me once—someone who had lived the streets, taken the meth, and stolen the car—that most of these people don't need to be there. Many are living the results of their own lack of discipline.

But it haunts me. Who are they, and why are they there? And didn't Jesus come for me when I was living the results of my own chosen sin? Didn't He come right down, not just to sit with me, but to *live with me?*

Today, I decided to bring desire into reality and go see these people. Join my friends who dish out food on hot Sunday afternoons, who walk where they walk, who reach out hands to ladle substance onto plates in hopes that love will reach far past food right into the heart.

I pass by well-suited men surrounded with ladies in skirts walking out of lovely church buildings, and my heart aches. It seems a bit artificial in light of who Jesus was, how He had nowhere to lay His head, how He sat with sinners.

Why do we ignore the hurting, the smoke-laden atmospheres, while following outward patterns of religion?

Is our religion even real at all, if we don't do what He did?

I cross the room to sit across from the girl in black with haunted eyes. She moans in pain of body, then verbalizes her pain of soul. She speaks of killing, of wondering which sequence is worse—homicide then suicide, or suicide then homicide. I listen, then mention gently that neither are good options, and the heart who does either has forgotten that each soul has purpose here on earth.

She moans again. Her bladder is infected and her purse has been stolen, she has no charger for her phone, and her husband (who looks thirty years older than she) has had his life threatened.

The kids I brought, the ones growing quickly toward teen years, sweep rounds across the floor and listen, ears perked. I know they are learning more here, right here in this place, than they will in ten Bible lessons at home in that clean living room with windows facing the water.

All is peace there; all is not peace everywhere in the world, and they need to see it, need to sweep that floor, need to carry melon to the table for more hungry bodies. They need to know first hand how much Christ needs them to be His hands and feet.

I bend low and hand over some money for the medication she needs for her infection. I warn her, low and quiet, that she must use it for meds and gas rather than drugs. She nods.

We pull away into sunlight, Walmart, crafts, and projects. It all seems trite, meaningless in light of the feast my heart just experienced. *I got to sit with them instead of drive by them.* It was like coming home, and tears spilled from my eyes as I realized my heart felt more satiated, satisfied, after sitting in that hot, smoky room than it does when I'm focusing on pleasure and *things.*

I can't believe how we run about life as if our resources were the end of all things. How we ignore the deep and replace it with the surface, all in the name of One who didn't have a place to call home, but made it His greatest prerogative to seek out, love, save the wounded.

As my friend Cody Joshua says, *"Remember, do not confuse the means with the end. As faithful stewards, we are to use these resources to fulfill our purpose. The resources themselves were never meant to become our purpose."*

Let's trade in our dissatisfied, living-for-the-surface type of life for one drenched in things vital to Christ, eternity, and love. Friends, let's be real in our quest for God and not be content until we live as He lived and walk as He walked, until we sit with them, catch their tears, spoon food onto plates and love into hearts.

Let's not play church, let's live Christ.

"Lord, help us to remember that you are only interested in the kind of religion that feeds the poor, visits the sick, and lives as you did. Cause us to know there is no true religion apart from yourself."

DAY 72

"Behold, I will bring to it health and healing, and I will heal them and reveal to them abundance of prosperity and security." Jeremiah 33:6, ESV

The crash was loud in the bookstore, and my eyes bounced quickly from my book to the merry eyes of an elderly lady. "Well," she says, "It didn't break!"

I smiled and then I couldn't help myself. "If that was me, I wouldn't have smiled. Thank you so much for your example."

Her eyes twinkled and I'm sure she thought to herself how many life lessons young ladies like me have to learn. Lessons like not expecting perfection in public. Of not thinking the world stops when you're the cause of an enormous crash in a giant bookstore. Of smiling when you want to disappear instead.

She chattered happily with her husband (what a lucky guy), and soon passed me by with a cheerful, "Merry Christmas!"

In that short exchange, my brain reeled with chances to apply what I just observed. I learned to laugh in an embarrassing moment; to give myself grace to make mistakes; to not think my worth is based on how well I perform. To just be happy.

Because doesn't the world need joy instead of perfection?

Cinderella may not be your name, and you may not have a castle. You may think you are not beautiful, that your life is nothing like a princess's and most certainly nothing like a fairy tale.

But you are a daughter. And I wish that all daughters knew what God says about them. If they did, they would hate themselves less even when others do, and would exist in a state of quiet confidence. They would quit staring in the mirror willing that large nose to turn into a smaller one, or those eyes to fade into a misty blue instead of brown.

They most certainly would not look to mankind for their approval; they would not flirt and flaunt with a hundred different men, because they have no need for that kind of attention. They know whose they are, and what kind of worth they have.

Fairy tales. You know, those were based on the deepest longings you hold in your heart as a woman. Filmmakers know humanity well and score millions of dollars by pulling on the strongest heartstrings.

They know what we sometimes don't know until we sit and watch their productions, and suddenly find ourselves crying over some "silly" movie for kids.

When that happens, don't dismiss yourself as some hopelessly childish adult who should be more mature. Embrace those desires, turn to Jesus, and realize that is exactly how you are loved by Him (and even better). Accept His pronouncement of you, that you are indeed a princess of even greater worth and loved more deeply than any film could portray.

Viewing yourself as loved, precious, a princess, even, will change your world. It will make you lovely, it will make you lovable. It will loose you from any bondage of rejection or insecurity you may still have. And, it will enable you to toss aside those areas in your life that are unbecoming to a princess.

In Christ, you are not only a daughter, you are a princess!

"Lord, thank you that knowing our true identity helps us not to cringe when we fear the disapproval of others. Today, help us to live, laugh, and love well."

Day 73

"But God forbid that I should boast except in the cross of our Lord Jesus Christ, by whom the world has been crucified to me, and I to the world." Galatians 6:14, NKJV

There's a trend among Christian women, a teaching that we need to be self-aware and self-confident, realize we are a princess, loved and adored by our Father. All this is true, and I've written about these things in this book.

But may I propose that we cannot be healthily confident without first fully acknowledging our own sinfulness and depravity apart from Christ? We cannot shed the things that hinder our confidence without acknowledging them in repentance.

Many times, what makes us insecure is knowing our sins and weaknesses. To rise above them, to have them crucified, we must bring them to Christ in full awareness of our need, and ask for His life.

We hear a lot about being secure in who we are, but may I suggest that *it is not so much about being secure in who we are, as in being secure in who Christ is.*

We need not so much feel in awe of ourselves as to be in utter awe of Christ. When Christ saturates our hearts, He washes our sinfulness and brings freedom of soul, which in turn breathes confidence and security because of who He is.

Insecurity becomes a foreign invader when Christ brings all He is to our hearts.

It won't work to tell yourself you are a princess without entering the narrow gate that allows you to become one. In John Bunyan's *The Pilgrim's Progress* we read of Christian, who had to enter the narrow gate in order to begin the journey. As he walked along he met another who had climbed over the wall to begin the journey, but was unable to continue in the journey because his entrance was not through the gate.

So it can be with us; we want the benefits without first bowing low. *We want to feel good about ourselves without first realizing we need to be rescued from ourselves.* We want to feel good about ourselves when Christ says there is none good, and in order to find life we must first die.

Women who are insecure as to their standing in Christ are often told to believe that they are washed and clean. Trying to tell yourself you are washed and clean, when in fact you've allowed sin to reign unchecked and unrepented of is counterproductive and may be the cause of ongoing doubt and insecurities.

You may try your whole life to have faith in yourself, but only faith in Christ will give you peace. And when you have faith in Him, you get to move beyond yourself and reckon yourself dead to sin.

Rather than telling yourself you are clean when you are not, remind yourself that Christ is clean and He promises to cleanse you the moment you come to Him. It is His goodness, His awesomeness, His grace that brings peace to your soul. If insecurities continue, continuously come to Him for His promised goodness and cleansing. Believe in it, rest in it—and you will find yourself secure, by coming to Christ for His promised cleansing.

"So Jesus said to him, 'Why do you call me good? No one is good but one, that is, God" (Luke 18:19, NKJV).

If the Son of Man refused to accept the title of good when He was truly good, if He wanted to hand the praise over to the Father, why do we want to feel good about ourselves apart from Him?

It's a bit like the child who was seen on his iPad in front of an eight-hundred-foot, giant, red oak tree. He was unaware of the beauty surrounding him while focused on something of so much lesser value. *So we, when we focus on feeling good about ourselves but lose sight of the only true goodness of the Father, lose out on worship and freedom.*

"Lord, thank you that true confidence can only come when we are first God aware. Help us to so appreciate you that we allow you to live in us, doing away with lies and sin that would otherwise drag us down."

"He has shown you, O mortal, what is good. And what does the Lord require of you? To act justly and to love mercy and to walk humbly with your God." Micah 6:8, NIV

You step on one child's toe and she says, "I'm sorry." She assumes that since there is difficulty, it must be her fault. She must have been in the wrong place at the wrong time.

The next child will be the one stepping on someone's toe, and instead of apologizing for it, will yell out, "Why are people always in my way?" She assumes that since there is difficulty, someone (and it's not her) must be messing up her life.

Daily, I work on the one child to admit her wrongs, to quickly apologize instead of spouting an accusation off the top of her head.

I remember sitting in a room of women who were opening up about sexual abuse. I was shocked to discover that nearly all of them had past issues they were wading through. Some of them still had not come out and dealt with the offense. They still thought that humility and forgiveness meant covering up for him.

This is the type of woman who apologizes when her toe is stepped on. She feels guilt instead of anger, forgetting that being angry with sin is also an attribute of God—and there's no guilt for someone else's wrong

I listened quietly, then could contain myself no longer. As best I could, I tried to help one dear lady see that covering up for the offender only keeps him in bondage as well. That forgiveness does not mean condoning. That real love brings the sin to light. That she is worth more than being used for another. That she could be free from the burden by coming out with the sin.

Women bow under heavy burdens for a duration of many years, only to destroy themselves and allow their offender to stay in captivity himself. This is not redeeming love, humility, or forgiveness.

I do not mean to say a woman can never allow a long-ago, childhood offense to dissolve without digging up the past. There may be times where healing occurs and one is confident of the healthy state of the past offender. But you must care for your heart and make sure healing comes.

Whenever you find yourself gasping for air just to live, when you feel stripped of your dignity, when life doesn't feel bright anymore, please take note and care for your heart. If it's something another is doing, don't feel the need to hide it. Acknowledge your own offense if there is any, repent of your own sin if you have any, but do not keep bowing under the misuse of another.

Those of you who've bowed under the weight of sexual abuse must reach out and bring it to light, at least to another loved friend. Your heart may well break if you don't. Or there may be a myriad of negative things in your life that you have no idea are connected to the pain from many years past.

True humility is able to rise to the occasion and acknowledge our own worth. Humility does not mean we allow another to misuse us, because somehow it must be our fault. Humility does not mean demoralizing ourselves—in fact, true humility is humble enough to see oneself as God sees us, as beings of incredible value and a people to be treated with excellence.

True humility is a balance between the girl who yells when *she* steps on someone's toes, and the girl who apologizes when her toe is stepped on. It is a healthy balance of kindness, and courage to also care for her own needs.

Devaluing oneself is, in fact, a twisted form of pride because we are so consumed with ourselves that we are rendered useless to the cause of justice, mercy, and love.

"Lord, thank you that you are a God of justice
as much as you are a God of mercy."

Day 75

"And he preached, saying, 'After me comes he who is mightier than I, the strap of whose sandals I am not worthy to stoop down and untie.'" Mark 1:7, ESV

John knew he was called, and he went. He knew his role was to prepare the way for someone greater than himself, and he found complete peace and purpose in that, though in the end, his head was sliced off because some wicked woman hated his words.

He was stripped of his dignity, his freedom, his very life, but he fulfilled his calling, and he did it well.

We have only to know what Jesus asks of us. Sometimes that "knowing" is as simple as a still, small voice letting us know what we are born to do. Other times, we may need to come out with deep personal needs and let go of that comforting blanket of our own make-believe perfect persona.

Letting go strips us and causes us to really live for God's promotion instead of our own. We have nothing to hang on to, nothing to portray, nothing to promote except Jesus.

For John, this was his reason to breathe. I have to believe he was willing to be stripped and let it all go if that meant promoting the life of Christ. And we, when we learn to be real and let it all out, end up promoting Christ even more than before because others see the mess, and then, they see the grace.

If they saw no mess, they would not rejoice in big, wild, free grace as deeply.

Letting go can be deflating if we've lived for years with the desire to impress. Sometimes people find meaning in giving impressions and when that is removed, they feel lifeless and flat. Here, though, is where true life begins. It is here, low at the cross, that God will minister true life to your spirit.

When we are humiliated because of our own sin or failure, we have a choice—allow the stripping to make us so grateful for Jesus' love that we become an even greater source of life than before, or go down because we cling to our own persona rather than to Christ.

Being stripped is a good thing. You may feel low, you may feel terrible, but you are in a good place. Listen carefully to God's words to you, and you will find fresh, vibrant life grow in your heart. After a while, you will so rejoice in your inner soul that you won't really care what people think anymore.

And because you have your mind on what God says to you instead of what people think of you, you are in a place to be internally drenched with goodness and peace.

Jesus asks us in John 5:44, "How can you believe, who receive honor from one another, and do not seek the honor that comes from the only God?"

It is so vital not to seek our own glory, that Jesus tells us we will even have difficulty believing when we are taken with ourselves.

"Lord, help us to absorb your worth to the extent it renders us willing to suffer and die for you if the need arises."

DAY 76

"'God opposes the proud but gives grace to the humble.' Humble yourselves, therefore, under the mighty hand of God so that at the proper time he may exalt you . . ." 1 Peter 5:5–6, ESV

Speaking of humility, I may as well fill you in on one of the most humbling experiences of my own life.

You might think this is silly, but for me, walking to the counselor's office was a painful walk of shame. Being seen walking toward the building was enough, but then I also had to open my heart to a near stranger.

There I was, mother and wife, by all appearances perfectly OK, but I was discovering that I couldn't figure life out on my own. I was, in fact, a mess.

I sat on the couch with tears streaming down my face and it all came tumbling out. It was humbling, but it was true.

How many of us grope along endlessly without finding what we're looking for? Does it have to take emotional exhaustion to get us to open up? Or, can we live a lifestyle of honesty?

Do we have to live for years with the same problems when someone may have wisdom to give us that will bring real change? Why do we choose to allow our mess to affect those we love when there's a way out, albeit humbling and painful?

The counselor looked at me and said, "So, you are a woman of great courage, aren't you?" And all I could do was shrug my shoulders slightly in sheer fright, and whisper, "I don't know. I hope so."

It takes courage to let go of your desire to appear perfect. It takes real bravery to live authentically. It's hard, but I would much rather live cleansed and whole than hang on to some performance mentality when Jesus says we shouldn't receive honor from others anyway. In fact, He asks how we can even believe when we want praise from people rather than Himself.

Humility has no persona to portray and is not worried about others' opinions of itself. When you're a mess, you're a mess. When you're not, you're not. Trying not to be when you are only turns you into someone fake—and no one is drawn to a fake person.

I found, as I opened up, that others loved me more, not less. They were there for me. Some of them shared their own hearts with me as a result of my transparency, because they felt safe.

When we open up and show the world we are every bit as human as another, we are drawn together in a common journey. We hold hands as we walk, rather than hope another is impressed by how far we've traveled.

I found more freedom that year than ever before. In letting go, I got to hold on. I held on to greater understandings of my own value in God's eyes, had greater capacity for joy, and was able to find wholeness in areas unknown to me before.

I let go of the desire to appear perfect, and found my desire for peace realized.

Reaching out, though thoroughly humbling, proved to lift the burden I was under. I share this because I believe many, many women strain under burdens they don't know what to do with, but are afraid to share with those who could help.

If you continue like this, damage will be done. You will either turn into an emotional disaster, or begin covering your heart in order to survive. (I did both.) No one is meant to do life alone.

If you are unable to find rest on your own with the Lord, go to a trusted friend, pastor, professional counselor, or, like I did, a combination. There is no shame in needing others in your life.

Unless you are an angel, a spirit, or God (and you are none of these), you will have many times where thoughts, advice, and prayers of other people will greatly enhance your life and help you find freedom.

Why do we think God created fellow human beings? For us to impress, or for mutual help and blessing? Instead of standing by observing others walk, we are meant to walk together. When one of us lags behind, the others are meant to pull us along.

I hear of pastors' wives living in a "fishbowl." Obviously, the pressure is great to live up to the standards that pastors and their families are called to. But here again, we must stop. In the Christian church, of all places, one need not pretend to be something they are not.

One pastor's wife literally fell on the floor in weariness so great she could no longer function. As others rallied around her, her husband was in another room entirely unaware. She was hiding her true heart to support her husband and her own appearance. It didn't work. *It never works.*

Sometimes, the church has more wounded, broken people leaving to find love than it has people staying to find healing. This should not be so. Where are those who know how to reach deep into the heart of an unlovable person to find out why she's like this? Where are the ones who take a repentant person and restore him or her back to fellowship even though the sin was great?

We become better at judging than we are at restoration.

It is much easier to mess up and back away, than to mess up and come back while wading through the difficult task of restoration. This is true for the offender and the offended as well.

Restoration is possible only when both parties are willing to do what it takes. If restoration is not happening, one party or another has something amiss. Often, it is both.

Humility is real. People need redemption because they are messy. How do we handle the mess? How do we handle our own mess?

"Lord, thank you that you always, without fail, give grace to the humble. Help us to flow, not flaunt. Help us give honor more than try to receive honor."

Day 77

"For do I now persuade men, or God? Or do I seek to please men?
For if I still pleased men, I would not be a bondservant of Christ."
Galatians 1:10, NKJV

A lone owl hooted somewhere off above the water, and I sat with my husband on a wet log, ears perked for noise, and the air so still it seemed as if the earth itself could hear me swallow.

I looked up. Gray everywhere, with trees tall and dark against the sky, leaves scattered across the damp earth of the forest floor. Something about the stately trees brought my soul in, and I felt as if I must wrap my arms about the width of the hard circumference. They were so real, just like they were created to be. I soaked it in.

And I wondered how humanity had dared to create for itself this fake existence when all the nature world still just was. You know, trees don't try to succeed for someone else's standard of success; they just grow tall because that's what they do.

That lone flower in the bare woods didn't try to be more beautiful than it already was. It didn't even want to move to a sunnier spot. It just bloomed there, pink and bright, hidden away where no one sees but the occasional hunter. (It didn't try to be less beautiful, or to hide its beauty, either.)

All the woods breathed contentment. Silent and still, just as it was.

I followed my man out of the darkness and turned on the car lights. Something inside me longed to stay there, build a fire, not shower for a day or two, see no one but the man beside me, of course. But civilization called me back to houses and lights and roads and cars and people. We are clouded over in a plastic existence we've dared create for ourselves, and few have the courage to be vulnerable, to be real, *to suffer the loss of popular thought for the richness of simple, yet solid, truth.* We feel compelled to earn more, more, and more so our families can consume more. We shop for clothes when our closets are already bursting with excess. Kids grow up with more emphasis on their accomplishments and performance than service and love. They are raised in a technological environment, which provides few opportunities to connect with nature.

Why must we walk deep into the woods and away from it all to feel our hearts connect with the real and unbiased? We all long to be accepted just as we are, to live in the real, to delight in the dusk and sunshine alike, to sing in the rain and dance in the shadows, to let our tears be seen and not only our joy. We should be allowed to have days where our hair is messy and our eyes tired, without worrying about our worth or other people's love and appreciation of us. *We long to see beauty as beauty is; not as a performance to perfect or a platform to build.*

Let the cars speed by and let others boast of success by gain; as for me, I shall learn my greater lessons from the trees, because they, unlike humans, exist how they were designed to be.

Let others take courage that they don't have to fit in to this crazy world, because really, we've built a shaky, unsustainable, unrealistic world to function in and judge ourselves by. Only the weak get sucked into the peer pressure of it all; the strong see past it and have core strength to return to all that really matters.

"Lord, deliver us from performance
and bring us to realness instead."

Day 78

"Her children rise up, and call her blessed. Her husband also, and he praises her.

"Many women have done excellently, but you surpass them all. Charm is deceitful and beauty is vain, but a woman who fears the Lord is to be praised.

"Give her of the fruit of her hands, and let her works praise her in the gates." Proverbs 31: 28–31, ESV

I am a mother of four young children. Any mama reading this will know that my days are maxed out with small things and it is easy to feel desirous of bigger, "better" accomplishments. It takes letting go, embracing the small in order to find the delight I am looking for.

It takes humility to realize that each mundane moment leads us right into eternity.

Jesus lived thirty years in mundane moments before branching out to a call greater than any we could know. He came to redeem the world, to be the savior, and still He embraced the small as long as He was here.

I have to believe He brought life and love into each ordinary day.

In the kingdom of Christ, the way up is the way down.

To become lowly, to rejoice in the small, brings us right to the throne room. It makes us part of His master plan.

Beautiful women are joyful women; joyful women are those who release the desires of their hearts and find worship on a daily basis. A mother of small children who radiates joy is one of the greatest testimonies of divine grace.

Mothers, may we grab hold of this! We are part of the divine order of things. Our role is immensely important, because raising children to be useful, God-honoring, purposeful adults is a great mission.

You hold in your hands an eternal soul.

Women who feel useless because of staying home fail to see the magnitude of their importance in the grand scheme of things.

This morning I was dismayed at the messiness of the kids' rooms. I have told them multiple times to clean them well *before* breakfast. Though it's easy to be frustrated with giving time to such a small thing, my thoughts wing forward to the future. Will my sons become disastrously messy men who can't pick up after themselves? Will they have piles of junk strewn about their yards or be unwilling to help out wherever they are?

The world is full of disaster, much of which relates to how a child was raised. Our job as mothers is to raise responsible, orderly adults. So, as I took time to teach my daughter how to make the bed well (again), I knew it was for a greater purpose.

Seeing the purpose of what we do as mothers gives us those wings we need to fly. Live each moment well, and you will have no past to regret and no future to dread.

It takes humility to embrace each day when little recognition is given for our effort. Most people don't rave over a mother's efforts of sweeping floors, changing diapers, and reading stories. But, *a humble woman needs no recognition to know her value.*

Imagine for a moment the difference in society if women threw their hearts into their families. Teaching a daughter to clean the bathroom well results in a grown woman who brings cleanliness and order to her world.

Helping your son grasp the math problem at hand is part of raising a man who may use his mind for great things. Cooking nutritious meals and teaching self-discipline to kids on a daily basis would drastically lower the amount of obesity and cancer in our society.

Developing a daughter's articulate brain through her childhood may enable her to become a doctor who will save lives.

Reading biographies to children can give them a vision of what God wants to do in the world and make them want to be a part of it.

"The hand that rocks the cradle rules the nation," said Abraham Lincoln. And may I add, we shape nations, reduce the rate of crime in our society, and raise pastors, doctors, hardworking men and women, and those who can love well.

Humility revels in the important whether seen, or unseen.

"Lord, thank you that there is meaning in each mundane moment; that mothering is not in vain; that each day is part of what it takes to lead our little ones back to yourself."

DAY 79

*"But whoever would be great among you must be your servant,
and whoever would be first among you must be slave of all.*

*"For even the Son of Man came not to be served, but to serve,
and to give His life as a ransom for many." Mark 10:43–45, ESV*

I drove along the Pennsylvania countryside and wondered at the vast number of churches populating the area. I thought of our own church back home in Washington state. I thought of the desire many Christians have for successful ministry, and I wondered . . .

If the universe is this vast, and Christians in every part of the world focus on their own ministry "success," isn't that using God?

I can see using vocation, career, or personal success as a means of feeling good about one's self, but using God? Aren't we supposed to worship God for His own goodness' sake? It has nothing to do with us appearing successful, or not.

My heart recoiled at the thought of Christ looking down to busy, occupied Christians much too focused on success in the name of numbers, well-attended services, and invitations to minister. Patting themselves on the back when the crowd attends or when they are asked to speak.

We have it all twisted. We use God, when we should be used by Him, for Him.

Falling in love with Jesus means you know *you are a small part of the universe, a very small part of the grand story God is writing, and you need no promotion in His kingdom because it's really not about that at all.*

You live your life based on what Jesus does *inside you.*

The fact that He loves on people we cut out of our lives impresses me deeply.

We may sit all day and discuss how legalistic certain groups of people are, but Jesus visits them and enters each heart who trusts Him. He is not ashamed to dwell in the heart of any person who receives Him, to be seen in their eyes, and be felt in their presence.

We may back away from a homeless person, but Jesus hovers near, waiting to enter and change a life.

We may never enter a bar to bring love there, but the Holy Spirit does, entreating hearts to find His peace rather than search for it in a bottle.

We may scorn the ill-behaved child, but Jesus will beckon and call to his heart all through his life.

We may judge another for not living out certain doctrines we hold dear, and all the while forget that we probably don't see or live something God has yet to show us.

We forget that Paul, who was struck blind with light on his way to imprison more Christians (he was that important to God), preached only the gospel of John for thirty-two years. There were some serious gaps in his teaching. When Priscilla and Aquilla heard him, they took him aside and explained the full gospel of Christ to him. Look at the patience of Christ in Paul's life.

We become a bit like Sarah in Genesis 21:10, who said "Cast out this bondwoman and her son, for the son of this bond woman shall not be heir with my son, namely with Isaac." She didn't know that the same God who loved her and gave her a son would also minister to, and keep alive, Hagar's son after she cast him out to die.

She didn't know that Ishmael was part of the greater story God was writing, and that a certain Jesus would enter the world hundreds of years later to redeem all people to Himself, without respect of persons.

We can be like Michal, who despised her husband for worshiping God in a linen ephod when she thought it shameful (2 Samuel 6). God freely accepted David's praise because he was beside himself with joy over what God had done, while Michal stood by in judgment.

And all the while, the Son of Man walks the face of the earth to see whose heart is toward Him. He never stops short or stays away from a hungry heart. He never breaks a bruised reed or quenches smoking flax, but heals and lights aflame those who look for Him.

People in the pews, is it really church if we're not doing the same? Does God care how big your building is, how successful your programs are, or how well attended your services are?

I daresay He doesn't. He walked among people, for people, had no elaborate building, but was so full of love that crowds followed him to the shore where He showed them even more of Himself. Without sending them away for their own food or berating them for coming unprepared, He fed them, healed their sick, and raised their dead.

As we drove home from a church service one day, I mentioned to the kids that I wanted to begin helping out with feeding the homeless. They reminded me that we had once heard a friend tell us that many on the street—including himself—were there because they chose to be.

I searched for the correct words for these little people who wanted to love on others, but needed to know it was worth the sacrifice. "Kids, we don't love on others because they are doing everything right. These people may or may not need to be there, but they do need Jesus. We can share Christ with them much better when we share life with them, share food with them."

Jesus didn't rebuke the mothers who sat at his side for three days, unprepared to be away from their homes. He didn't tell them it was their own fault they were weak with hunger. He didn't even say that to the strong men in the crowd. Rather, He stayed with them and showed love, not only by preaching truth but by ministering to each need.

His hands-on love verified the credibility of His message.

As in Revelation 3:2, we also may have a reputation for being alive when we can be dead. As we walk across paved church parking lots in heels and lovely dresses to a crowded building, we may look very much alive when in fact, we are dead.

How much of Jesus do we have in our hearts, and how well do we bring His love to others? In essence, this is what matters most, because this is what Jesus came to be and do for those He loved. When He left this earth, He gave the task to us.

Anything else or less will shame the name of Christ and hinder, not draw, others to Himself. People would rather you sit where they sit, see what they see, and show them Christ than watch you perform on a Sunday morning. We may say they are spiritually dead, when in fact, Jesus may look on us and pronounce us dead while we think we live.

People in the pews, before you raise your hands, make sure you've also bowed your heart and succumbed to the Love that came to reach all, encompass all, and redeem all.

The Son of Man walked humbly, and showed mercy.

> *"Father, help us not to use you for our purposes,*
> *but allow you to use us for yours."*

Day 80

". . . for I have learned in whatever situation I am to be content. I know how to be brought low, and I know how to abound. In any and every circumstance, I have learned the secret of facing plenty and hunger, abundance and need. I can do all things through him who strengthens me." —Philippians 4:11b-13, ESV

She called me that day. "Sara, can we go to the park? And we could get coffee if you want."

I heard her childlike voice and pictured this delightful, handicapped, forty-year-old lady holding her phone to her ear in eagerness to get out for fun and sunshine. How could anyone say no?

The kids and I were going to catch up on housework that day. All the windows were to be washed inside and out and so much more was on my to-do list. But at that moment I knew my day would change, and it would be good.

We pulled up to the espresso stand and my dear friend said she wanted a chocolate milk shake. As I handed it to her, she thanked me and dove right in. The humility in what had just happened struck me.

There was no guilt in desiring something. No pressure to feel like she needed to pay for her treat.

There was unashamed pleasure, just like that of a child, in something she did not provide.

Simple asking, simple receiving, simply being blessed, and in turn, blessing my day.

Spending time with Mari is pressure free. She does not perform, so neither do I. We spent that hour together, just being. It felt great.

I want to be like Mari. I don't have to be perfect, and neither do those around me. Accepting that I will not always hit perfection, I find grace to forgive others when they mess up as well. Why do we think performing well is such a big deal?

If I love like a child loves, I will forgive quickly. I won't think in circles about my own mess-ups until I feel upset to my stomach. I will live and laugh and love others until they feel safe with me. They know I am not about their perfection, but about their hearts experiencing grace and love when they are with me.

Humility is the "state or quality of being humble in spirit; freedom from pride and arrogance. An act of submission or humble courtesy." (Webster's Collegiate Dictionary, 1898)

God only desires us to walk in what He has given; how we measure to others is of no value at all. Our value comes from the fact that God formed us and gave us what He wanted to give. Seeing this frees us from comparison and discontentment; it also frees us to flourish freely in the gifts God has given us.

And you don't need to wow people with anything—you just need to live Christ in everything.

Discontentment in who God made us to be is false humility. Holding back on our gifts for fear that others will judge us as prideful is also false humility.

The only rightful place for us to be is deep contentment

and delight in what God has given us, and maximizing our potential to the fullest.

Humility is not hanging around the corners of a room when God has given you a love for people and a gift to draw them out. Humility is not worshiping on the back pew of a church if God wants to use you up front.

It is not humility to hold back your gifts so that others will be comfortable and not envious. That, in all reality, is fear and pride. It is consciousness of what others think more than what God delights in and wants to do in you.

Jesus is looking over the face of the whole earth to see if there is a heart free from thoughts of self. If He can use a person greatly and still get all the praise, if there are those willing to be in the forefront as well as serve in hidden places, knowing there is no difference in the kingdom of heaven?

Will He find a heart cleansed and free from concern of those things at all? Pure hearts who realize that kingdom greatness is not as the world views greatness?

It is silly to compare ourselves with our fellow created humans when each of us has been specifically made for a certain purpose. We have no accomplishments or glory to gain. We have no "low" or "high." We only live out what He put in.

As others do the same, we do not judge them as the world judges. We don't put labels on others by what they accomplish or do. We simply love all God creates in a person, and desire each one to maximize their gifts to the fullest potential.

Any gift, beauty, or goodness in another is God's goodness displayed for His glory. When we envy others, we do not really envy them—rather, since it is His handiwork, displayed for His pleasure, we are grasping at God's goodness, wanting to make it our own.

Their very breath is given to them and they would cease even to live, should He choose not to grant another.

Envy reminds me of what Lucifer did, when he was an angel but wanted to be equal with God. He grasped at the very magnificence, all for his own glory. *Wanting greatness or beauty that God placed in another is trying to steal the greatness of God for our own glory.*

We don't usually think of it in this way. We get people oriented, people focused, and forget that it's all God, His creation, His possession, His passion *displayed in various ways for a story much larger than ourselves.*

"Lord, help us be content with what you've given us and cultivate those gifts to their maximum potential."

Day 81

"Do not be afraid. Stand firm and you will see the deliverance the Lord will bring you today. The Egyptians you see today you will never see again.

The Lord will fight for you, and you need only to be still." Exodus 14:13–14, ESV

I pressed my head against the window and stared into the fresh morning, sun rising in hues of pink over silent water. Living on the bay offers so much feasting for the eyes it makes the heart go still.

This morning, though, it comes alive.

Yesterday I sat on the shores of the lake watching the boys play with their daddy while I read Staci Eldridge's bestseller for women, *Captivating*. I closed the pages understanding just a bit more of my own heart.

She says we want to be fought for, be rescued, be loved so passionately that, like Cora in *The Last of the Mohicans*,[1] we have a hero whispering in our ear, "No matter how long it takes, no matter how far, I will find you!"

---

1   *The Last of the Mohicans*. Directed by Michael Mann. US: Morgan Creek Productions, 1992.

I guess this is why I love when my husband walks into the bedroom where I lay sick on the bed, and pulls out one chocolate bar after another with a grin. I know he dislikes shopping and he's short on time, but he brings what I need, and he brings not one, but seven. Or when I'm cold and he wraps his great big arms around me, runs home, and returns with blankets and coats for all of us.

There may be no French and Indians to keep at bay in our world, but just the same, he fights for me. And as I stare into the sunrise with my heart lifted up, I know that Christ is all of that, too.

He came for me, He pursued me, He faced the powers of darkness and hell so I could be rescued. The world stopped and went black when He gave His life for me. Then, because He didn't want me to be alone, He rose again and gave me His Spirit while He goes to be with His Father. He's preparing a place for me, there, and will come again for me.

He didn't just defy glistening blades and deafening gunpowder, He defied the very powers that have broken the hearts of women ever since the serpent deceived our sister Eve in the Garden. There is so much more for Him to conquer than for any other hero, and His victory is certain.

In fact, He's already won it, and you have only to receive His relentless, passionate love.

He's strong, He's able, and He wants to be the one to fight so you don't have to. This is why He says our strength lies in confidence and quietness. Why He asks us to stand still so we can see the salvation of the Lord. Why He says that faith, not striving, is the shield that will ward off every single dart of the enemy.

He's our Hero. The greatest One we will ever know. His love makes the heart stop, beat fresh, and then come alive.

Fellow sisters, women, girls who long to be pursued and fought for, today may you realize that the most valiant hero ever named fights for you and is not content until you are resting in His bosom. You may meet Him, trust Him, and allow your heart to go still in realization that you are the beauty in a story greater than any you could read of, and Christ is your relentless pursuer who won't be satisfied until He has you.

"Lord, thank you that you fight for me. Thank you that the Spirit intercedes for me, and I am fought for with the greatest power known in heaven or earth."

DAY 82

"There is therefore now no condemnation to those who are in Christ Jesus.

"For the law of the Spirit of life has set you free from the law of sin and death." Romans 8:1–2, ESV

Many times, we struggle earnestly to loose some grip, to gain victory in a certain area of weakness. But all too often, we struggle in vain. The grip never loosens and we spend years trying to shed a certain problem.

One day I was in such a dilemma. I loved Jesus, and wanted to walk upright before Him. But victory seemed short lived, and always, I found myself struggling and failing in the same area as before.

Why do many Christians claim the blood of Jesus in earnest and sincere repentance, but find little or no relief from the battle within? I've seen believers fast, pray, ask for counsel, and still gain no peace *while others grasp ahold of grace and walk with a certain triumph of soul that breathes confidence and peace.* What is the difference?

Our faith in Christ is not in understanding everything about Christ; our faith is based on who Christ says He is.

I remember being acutely aware of my own sin and need

of a savior when I was fourteen years old. I knelt, in tears, and accepted Jesus' forgiveness. But since I had little awareness of the power of trust, I continued in my own struggle against that sinful nature constantly vying for my allegiance.

I remember wanting to feel love rather than hatred. I also remember the dear friend who looked at me and said, "Because Jesus loves them, and you are his child, you can also love them regardless of what you naturally feel."

It didn't click. Not until many years later did I fully grasp the depth, beauty, and renewal of faith.

I realized that rather than struggle for victory, I needed to remember who Jesus said He was. He declares me free. He declares me whole. Not because I asked Him in faith for forgiveness years ago, but because *today, each day, all day is a walk of trust for the believer.*

We cannot try to be holy any more than we were able to save ourselves initially. That bitterness you feel toward someone will not disappear by trying to feel love.

Now, when I feel the battle of my own nature within me, I look up. I then become convicted of righteousness. *Because I have the witness of His Spirit through faith, I become fully aware that the righteousness of Christ is mine to possess.* Conviction of righteousness becomes so strong that it dims whatever else I may be experiencing.

I once spoke with a dear friend who felt guilty for wanting praise from people, who felt less than adequate, less gifted, and less accomplished than others. She wanted to focus only on Christ's thoughts of her, but continued in a relentless battle to do away with her desire for human affirmation.

I was listening to a sermon when it hit. And though the speaker was entirely engaging on one of my favorite topics,

I could only bend low over my paper and pour out what the Lord was speaking to my heart. In essence, this is what I wrote:

Fighting the desire for praise from people is much less productive than receiving the worth and honor Christ gives us. He created you for you, because He wanted you. This is why we should never try to duplicate another. Doing so makes us tense and unnatural, which in turn distracts us from giving 100 percent to the gifts God gave us.

Whatever you naturally do well is the gift God has given you.

A runner doesn't need to force himself to run like someone who is not born for it will need to.

A singer doesn't have to try to sing; rather, if she doesn't sing, she feels like something's missing. A writer feels devoid of life when she doesn't write. Someone who is gifted with hospitality loves to host and serve. That is simply who they are because God made them that way.

He wants you to replicate the value He bestows on you. You are worth the life of His son. Feeling inadequate and ungifted is a false sense of humility. *A good Creator never designs an ungifted creature; rather, you join the masses of others created to display His honor.*

We greatly dishonor our Creator when we are dissatisfied with what He made.

Seeing Jesus, seeing His creation in ourselves and being in awe that He should honor us with His name causes us to worship in the core of our being. We fall in love with Him more than we fall in love with what we think He will do for us

Others become mere fellow humans whom we hold lightly because the Presence of Greatness enraptures our hearts. *We become so alive with what He has said, that our own emotional and spiritual drama pales in comparison.*

Things that used to tense us up become an avenue for grace.
Sometimes we fight with the wrong weapons. We try not to feel a certain way. Much more is gained by absorbing truth and allowing the light of it to change our hearts. The truth sets us free. *The conviction of righteousness is greater than the conviction of sin because the power of love always wins.*

Just because Jesus lives, just because He came, just because He remains that Sacred Presence to romance our hearts. *We were designed to remain in the center of the Trinity.*

The presence of darkness reveals an absence of light, and our hunger to break free is a call from God to come in, to abide, to wash away the conviction of sin with the stronger conviction of His righteousness.

Truth is more powerful than sin, and love always wins. Godly sorrow leads to repentance that *allows love to win by reason of its greatness.* For the believer, this can happen the moment you realize your fallen nature is rising. You can and must immediately look up and allow the even greater conviction of the powerful righteousness of your Father to let you know who He is, and who He promises to be to you if you trust Him.

The knowledge of who Christ is will do wonders more than the constant struggle of your own self to rise above sin or weakness. *Just as you were initially saved by faith, so you must walk each day.*

Christ never wants to be replaced. This is why redemption through faith in the sacrifice and righteousness of Christ happens not only once, but each and every day.

In the heat of the next battle, step aside quickly and ask yourself, "What does Jesus say to me?"

If you still feel low in faith and victory, ask yourself, "Who does Jesus say *He* is?"

You may have constant doubt as to your own standing with the Father, but you cannot doubt Christ's standing with His own Father and the fact that He promises His righteousness when you trust.

Trust is the most powerful weapon ever, and when engaged, will certainly wield deadly blows to your enemy. You are no match, but God is. You must not strive because you will not win; you will only wear out and become old with struggle.

But in the kingdom of heaven, there are only solutions. Since Christ is the only solution, it remains that trust in Him brings about surrender to His ways, a changed life, and deep rest.

"In returning and rest you shall be saved; in quietness and confidence shall be your strength" (Isaiah 30:15b, NKJV).

You must look away, and you must look *up.*

"Father, thank you that responding to your truth does more to refute lies than any of our own efforts. Help us to enter your rest."

Day 83

"*The integrity of the upright guides them, but the unfaithful are destroyed by their duplicity.*" Proverbs 11:3, NIV

I pulled and prodded on that stubborn thing. It was going to come out, one way or another.

The screwdriver buried into the wood and made dents, but still it stuck fast. Staples and hooks can be tenaciously stubborn. I dug this way and that, gouging even deeper into varnished wood that should stay intact.

Suddenly it flew out, straight into my son's face. He yelled, and it disappeared onto the floor somewhere hidden beneath the rocker it was dug from. That broken hook was gone, never to tear at my rocker cushions again, especially not the new ones I had sewn that day. They were beautiful, and the tearing had to end, today.

As I worked, my life felt much the same. So much digging had been done that year. It hurt to dig deep, to uncover, to pull out nasty hooks in my heart. It was unpleasant for a while as we tried to pull out the troublesome hook. But in the end, the sharpness was gone and the tearing ceased.

Denial of our pain means we close the door to healing from it. Sometimes we need to do some uncomfortable digging in our hearts in order to bring peace. It is worth every bit of discomfort, and in the end, the cushion of your heart will cease to be torn.

God is all about your wholeness, not your tearing. He is out to pull up those sharp things so you can rest without destruction. Allow Him to dig deeply and pull up those things you don't want touched. Allow Him to pull, to prod, to dig it up and out. Covering up may seem helpful for a while, but it will always resurface until you allow God to pull it out.

As long as you avoid dealing with the sharp hook hidden underneath the cushions, you will be torn. It must be removed. Rather than spend a lifetime trying to deny it, turn your cushion over and allow the nasty tear to be seen. Then, allow it to be healed.

He stands there, and He offers healing to you. You are meant to be a woman of redemption!

"Father, thank you that in you, facing our sharp places makes us able to find healing."

DAY 84

"You keep him in perfect peace, whose mind is stayed on you, because he trusts in you." Isaiah 26:3, ESV

I listened, entirely taken with the vibrant young mama as she said, "I want to sing songs from my triumph and my sorrow, but all of it speaks of your nature."

She had a bone disease, not once, but twice. Life is difficult with a bone disease giving you rashes all over your body and rendering you helpless. As she fought, wept, and cried, she also accepted the good God was working in her.

Melissa Helser knows that God loves our "yes" in the valley or the mountaintop, and all that matters is that we say yes. She learned to understand God's character, which allowed her not to question His motives. Her song is one of my favorites, birthed from her heart of gold.

I don't have a bone disease, but I've had diseases of the heart that needed healing. Fear and insecurity can eat away at me with a vengeance, and, before I know it, I'm so taken with anxiety that my head feels thick. I worry about the friendship issues the kids may be having, and how to work it out without further offense. I worry that I won't mother well enough, be a friend who's present enough, or be the wife my husband needs.

Such was the state of my heart that morning when I knelt on the floor with worship music swirling around me.

I lifted my head upward, and in my mind's eye I saw a large Presence hovering above many smaller ones below. I knew it was God. I knew He was calling me to be taken with Him, to release what people may think or do so I could be taken with what He thinks and does.

Heaven came down, and I knew beyond doubt that it was God and me more than them and me.

The glory gates seemed to swing wide open there on that dining room floor as the sun rose over the bay and worship swelled through the little house. I will never forget that powerful word from my Father. It is God and me. It is God for me. It is God with me.

If, on the day of my death, I will be alone with my Father, I must also walk every single day hand in hand with Him. The heart raveled up tightly in a knotted ball unravels.

My heart unravels, there, and it unravels again the next Sunday as we sing it together. That prayer meeting, where we all gather round each other and I'm held by the shoulders and prayed for, does me in all over again. *He unravels me.*

But that morning as I worshiped on my knees, there was a pinch on my leg. I looked down, horrified to see an earwig pinching away at my skin. I brushed him off and he scurried away, but I wasn't satisfied. I picked him up and tossed him out. There's no room for him in this house.

So, dear friends, there's no room for what pinches and knots and ravels our minds when we see that it's God and us more than them and us.

"Lord, I love to be unraveled by you. Thank you for taking the knots and making them smooth."

Day 85

"The path of the righteous is level; You make level the way of the righteous.

"In the path of your judgments, O Lord, we wait for you.

"Your name and remembrance are the desire of our soul."
Isaiah 26:7–8, ESV

January ground is soggy and wet. Moss hangs on trees and all the world has been drenched for days, and a toad croaks loudly from some dark, drenched corner.

I stared at the sky. It was gray. I picked up garbage and scooped up mounds of dirt those nasty moles dug up around the yard, and as I drove out the driveway, it was muddy, too.

Even the bay was gray. A lone paddleboarder glided by, nearly covered in shrouds of mist, and a seagull hopped slowly across the road as if its blood was running as slowly as the sky was bleak.

But then I noticed the roses. Tall blossoms waited in covering leaves, ready to burst forth in color for the gray world to rejoice in. I was struck by the contrast. They dared blossom in this?

They didn't wait to blossom until the sun came out. They didn't wait to show color until the earth was baked in warmth.

They had no fear—they just blossomed because that's what they do.

They didn't care if anyone was out and about to see. They weren't afraid the cold would brittle up their tender, delicate petals. They weren't worried about losing their luster, their brightness. All they did was be roses—because that's what roses do.

So you, dear lady, were born to bloom. And don't ever allow anyone or anything to tell you otherwise, *because no one can stop you from being what you were born to be. No one, that is, but yourself.*

That weight you carry wasn't meant to be yours. Someone with big shoulders came to bear it for you if you will let Him.

The sorrow you bear will eat you up if you don't hand it over to that Someone who loves you with everlasting love.

The buoyant life you felt as a child is yours to retrieve—because that's who you are, because you are born with privileges no one has authority to take.

Acknowledge your pain so you can find healing from your pain.

Even the founding fathers knew that each person was born with unalienable rights, among them life, liberty, and the pursuit of happiness. Take that one step further and you will see that God, your God, your great, wise, good creator God says you are His daughter and He gives you joy in the midst of, and in spite of.

Allow Him to breathe it in your soul, and when He does, *you will rise as a lioness with prowess in all you do, because you know whose you are. You will feel yourself come alive, and when you do, you will smile in the dark and smile in sunshine because God never changes like the sky does.*

You will have sure footing.

You will stand strong.

You will thrive, because *that's who you were born to be, just as the rose was created to bloom.*

> "Father, help each daughter to see that it is her birthright to bloom. Help each of us not to allow anything to take our beauty away."

DAY 86

"You are the light of the world. A city that is set on a hill cannot be hidden. Nor do they light a lamp and put it under a basket, but on a lamp stand, and it gives light to all who are in the house.

"Let your light so shine before men, that they may see your good works, and glorify your Father in heaven." Matthew 5:14–16, NKJV

Jesus communicates confidence, and as He breathes confidence in you, He also calls you to create light, freedom, and glory.

Light cannot help but shine. True light will feed others and shed light on their souls and environment. *We are to change the atmosphere in which we live.*

Jesus filled His disciples to the point they were shaken, so they could go forth boldly. Not to hide the light He gave, but to manifest it so that the world would see the glory of God.

"To them God willed to make known what are the riches of the glory of this mystery among the Gentiles: which is Christ in you, the hope of glory" (Colossians 1:27, NKJV).

We manifest light by knowing the giver of lights. In the beginning, He created light, and He has been creating light in the hearts of men and women ever since. We get to know the light He gives when we see Him for who He is—incredibly glorious and beautiful.

We see Him as His own being, not somehow measured by what we experience in a fallen world. The world is fallen; God is not. Yet, people measure Him daily by circumstances, people, and things. God remains so much higher than all of these.

Blessed are those women who place their hope in a gloriously good Father who cannot be measured by fallen people or difficult circumstances. If Job had ceased believing during his trials, he would never have known the goodness of God. Little did he know that God was showing forth His greatness through Job's trials, and that Satan would have to bow his head in shame as he walked away.

We hold on to light when we cease holding on to people and become willing to experience gain or loss

Martyrs are not extraordinary Christians; they are ordinary Christians whose faith proved itself in ordinary circumstances.

In sorrow, we learn more of His comfort.

In joy, we realize that even happiness does not fill the heart as He does. We learn that He lives in a realm far above anything here, and that we need His newness of life to share the light He wants to give.

We see Him elevated, as supreme, as omniscient and omnipresent. In seeing these things, we worship Him as the author of hope for the hopeless, the giver of love for the unlovable, the forgiver of sins for the sinner, the comforter for those with breaking hearts, and the giver of life.

Seeing Jesus makes the heart come alive. We become more than benchwarmers in a church because when we see all this glory, we cannot help but share it. It becomes in us a river of living water, and rivers always *flow to bring nourishment to the world.*

When Christians display the light Jesus gives, they bring hope to others in darkness. Humility does not hide light that belongs to Jesus.

Jesus wants to shine!

In this world, nothing remains untainted; even a post you paint will lose its color. But God's people are changed from glory to glory when they see Jesus transcending all things, and learn to abide there.

God is never to be compared to our experiences here on earth—He is far above anything we could see, feel, touch, or experience. When we abide in who He is instead of what we experience, we finally, truly, take wings. *In this life, we bring glory because we abide in glory.*

Glory like this cannot help but shine!

> "Father, help us to be rivers of life to bring
> your nourishment into the world."

DAY 87

"Thus says the Lord who made you, and formed you from the womb, who will help you: 'Fear not, O Jacob my servant; and you, Jeshurun, whom I have chosen.

" 'For I will pour water on him who is thirsty, and floods on the dry ground; I will pour my Spirit upon your descendants, and my blessing on your offspring;

" 'They will spring up among the grass like willows by the watercourses.'

" 'One will say, "I am the Lord's;" another will call himself by the name of Jacob;

" 'Another will write with his hand, "The Lord's," and name himself by the name of Israel.'" Isaiah 44:2–5, NKJV

I drove through the well-populated state of Pennsylvania, and wondered at the countless churches occupying towns and cities. Each one had its own form of living out what they thought was Christ's heart for the world.

I pondered culture thoughtfully as we came upon one horse-drawn carriage after another on the winding roads of what they call Amish Paradise. On some faces, I saw peace. On others, a blank stare emerging from a heart caught in the endless beat of performance.

Later, I listened to my sister tell stories of Greece, and how God is reaching down to bring freedom into hearts who realize that Jesus brings peace and love after ISIS destroyed and killed their loved ones.

I encountered vastly opposing cultures in the week of travel, and in each one, there were faces blank and hopeless contrasted to those alight with peace.

That He should want to, choose to, dwell among people baffles me. We are so small in the vast universe, yet, He walks here, looking for those who really want Him.

He enters the heart of the former Muslim lady in Greece who is chatting with my sister.

He enters the heart of the Amish lady carrying yet another generation of canned goods down to her ancient cellar.

He calls on the heart of the radically diverse people sitting in that bus as it carries them to their destinations.

He is no respecter of persons. And as I felt small in the great, wide, population of the universe, I was incredibly grateful that He brings light and hope to all those who trust Him, regardless of their culture.

His hope enters us as we look up when we want to look down and around. He allows other hopes to vanish beyond our grasp so we become hungry enough to look to the Source of Hope, who then fills our hearts with more hope than we could ever know in other places.

When we are stripped bare, He fills us full. So full, that even our bareness becomes less barren because His fullness doesn't compare to anything earthly. As He fills us, then, life merges into true life, and we are changed.

Refuse to give the enemy gratification by wallowing in purposelessness and depression. God is always up to something when you feel you're down to nothing.

A young mama may feel depression over her present circumstances while a fifty-year-old lady despairs over what she feels are worthless years behind her.

A man who strives long for the vocation he wants may feel discouraged that his job is not the fulfillment of his deepest needs and desires.

The world over, people long for hope. Many feel the sense of "we eat, sleep, work, then get up to do it all over again." For what purpose?

Hope and purpose lie in believing God is creating a larger story, one that is bigger than us but that we are a part of. Our lives were literally created to be part of a grand story that is being written.

In the story of the world, God's children especially have a grand part to play. We are light bearers in the darkest parts of the story.

Picture the worst, most critical scene in a movie, in which the hero or heroine comes along to change the outcome of the helpless. Darkness and light flashes before our eyes on the screen. In some way, this is a small picture of the story of the world, and we get to be the ones sent to help, bring light, show love, and change certain parts of the play because of the mission we've been given by the Creator of the show.

It's not that we have to be here. It's that we get to. Ours is a vitally important existence. The lines are drawn in spiritual places, and we get to fight.

To be planned, formed, and created in the womb for a purpose to a loving God will bring us great hope. Life is not an existence to be survived as best we can—it is a beautiful gift waiting to be given back to the Lord, and the rest of the world.

We must know He delights in us! If we place much thought into making something for ourselves, we do so because we *want* it. **God literally wants us!** He has a plan for each individual life.

The One who formed you for Himself, who has called you with a purpose, is also the One who gives beauty for ashes, the oil of joy for mourning, and the garment of praise for the spirit of heaviness.

Women, there is great hope, great purpose, and much joy as we live in the kingdom! We know for whom we live.

"Lord, thank you that we never need feel purposeless, but can know we have a major part to play in the story you are writing. Help us only play our part well by giving in to you well."

Day 88

"She consider a field, and buys it. With the fruit of her hands she plants a vineyard." Proverbs 31:16, ESV

Women are born to create. Whether materially or spiritually, we are designed by God to bring good into this world.

Is this why I love to create something out of nothing? Why my grandma loves to paint, my mother finds immense satisfaction in gardening, and my sister totally enjoys sewing while her twin turns out the most amazing concoctions in her kitchen? Why my friend bursts with pleasure when her business-savvy brain pulls the pieces together to create a substantial flow of income?

We were born to bring life and beauty into this world, not only by giving birth, but by designing, creating, and making things.

This is why ladies rearrange furniture when their husbands think it a waste of time. Why they decorate their homes even if all they can afford are yard sale items instead of Pottery Barn. Why some of their greatest joys are finding a new dress on the clearance rack to bring beauty into the closet. Why some love to work out and find pleasant changes in their physique even if it takes time and energy.

The list is endless.

Even more than material accomplishments, we are meant to create goodness for the soul.

A child's first impression of life is warmth and tenderness from her mother. A teenager still often comes to his mother for food and comfort. A woman reflects the heart of God with sacrifice, giving, and being there unconditionally for those in her care.

If we love to meet every need of our child, how awesome it is to know that God wants us to need Him. It would pain us if our kids felt like they were too much by being honest with their needs, and in the same way, we honor God by asking Him for everything our hearts need.

How many times do we try to be self-sufficient? We try to have it all, do it all, be it all so He will think we're worthy. If our kids acted like that, we would think it ludicrous. Our reason for being there would be annihilated and our hearts grieved.

When you are weary of giving, remember you also have a Giver over you. Keep "buying your field and planting your vineyard." Refuse to become lifeless and dull.

The Ultimate Giver gives more life, love, and care than you could dream of being capable of giving. One who absolutely wants you to come for refreshing and joy. One who promises to fill your cup no matter what your day is like.

To represent such a God is an honor of the highest degree.

So keep giving life, creating, making beautiful your surroundings in whatever capacity you naturally function well in. Using the gift you have in natural things becomes spiritual when we see that everything in the world was created to bring glory to its Creator. Running your business, serving your family, painting, or decorating . . . all of it enhances God's world because we are functioning in His world in the ways He gifted us.

Love your life as a woman! Find someone to nurture, whether it be your neighbor, your child, a foster child, a refugee, or a lonely youth from your church.

Dare to reach out and past the walls of your own comfort. Life will become wild with meaning and your heart will soar because you were meant to create, both physically and spiritually.

Dare to create a safe haven for someone. Dare to risk, to do, to step out. Dare to be a woman who creates love, beauty, and goodness wherever she goes.

"Lord, thank you for giving us the ability to bring beauty into the world. Help us do that in our speech, actions, and lives."

Day 89

"*Better is a little with the fear of the Lord, than great treasure and trouble with it.*

"*Better is a dinner of herbs where love is, than a fattened ox and hatred with it.*" Proverbs 15:16–17, ESV

That look.

I saw it on his face as he chopped at the board vigorously, willing it to break. I heard his voice snap, just like mine does when the world seems too big for me to handle, and my nerves pop and my brain runs a thousand different directions, because I want to accomplish a thousand different things, *now.*

He tossed ferns on the floor of his fort and chopped at the board and asked his tired mama to haul firewood. He snapped at his brother and guzzled water and asked if we could stay and help longer. That intense drive toward accomplishment, of a job complete, was turning my boy into something other than his usual self.

By nature, he's calm and steady. Daily, I remind him that diligence and speed reward more than laziness. Not today. Today, he's driven.

Driven just like his mama has been for the past month, head bent low, putting in grueling hours to accomplish my goal. It's not been an easy month, and as it closes, my goal is finished but my heart is dry. As if I knocked myself around for something rather than for *someone.*

I wanted the thrill of accomplishment, and I went all out to get it even when my brain swirled and my eyes drooped and the heart went dry. Then, with my project complete, I stood there, wondering where the thrill was.

The thrill of accomplishment is overrated when we trade it in for the thrill of the God zone.

Stress is the assumption that more must be accomplished than we are well able to do. That we will be worth more, feel better about ourselves, even if it takes our health and peace in the process. That somehow, something other than Christ will satisfy when the sun goes down, the night is black, and we lay, pondering, while all is still.

Rather than dare ourselves to accomplish more than we can do with peace and grace, let's dare ourselves to slow down, to breathe, to enjoy the process. To love moments in the middle of the mess as much as we love the mess all cleaned up.

We eat, clean up; eat, clean up; then eat and clean up one more time. We stress over things we need to do for many years over because we've forgotten these moments are building lives, and that millions of others are doing the same things because living demands it. But it's not the end goal. If it were, stress would be understandable, perhaps even admired.

What if we spend our days enjoying the process just as much as we enjoy the accomplishment?

What if, rather than rush about with a furrowed brow, we hold the gift of today for what it is—a small part of life in a great big world where we all pitch in, and we all give, and we all breathe and live and love until eternity comes?

It must look sad, perhaps even humorous, to a great big God when He looks down and sees all of us rushing, like a swarm of bees or hill of ants, driven to the point of weariness and exhaustion. Snapping at His people, even. Making more so we can rush about and consume more, when all He wants is a quiet moment with us so He can speak straight into our hearts about what our lives are all about.

It's all about enjoying Him, and bringing others to enjoy Him, forever. As John Piper says, "God is most glorified when we are most satisfied in Him" (*Desiring God*, John Piper, 1986).

You cannot reach the end goal without living the moments, and moments are what culminate into a lifetime. *Extraordinary or mundane, they lead us all right into eternity.*

Friends, at the end of the day, our souls were made to dance to the eternal more than they were ever meant to rush about for *things*.

Today, enjoy your creations, but enjoy your Creator more!

"Lord, thank you for the ability to enjoy creating.
Help us to enjoy the process, because all good things
require a process. Help us honor you in the process,
long before we feel the accomplishment."

DAY 90

"And he also who had two talents came forward, saying, 'Master, you delivered to me two talents; here, I have made two talents more.'

"His master said to him, 'Well done, good and faithful servant. You have been faithful over little; I will set you over much.

"'Enter into the joy of your master.'" Matthew 25: 22 and 23, ESV

The two boys and I hopped into the minivan one Saturday morning, and as we pulled up to the first yard sale, I stared at an old black bookshelf with a hole in the side. Two houses converging into one, and they needed to get rid of *stuff*.

I bought it, hole and all. A few houses later I stood again, this time staring at an ancient wicker end table with chips of white paint flaking off. It must have been an eighty-year-old grandmother's table by the looks of it. But I saw potential, and I bought it.

You see, I had been praying for outdoor furniture, and saw this piece as an answer. We were paying off debt and I knew buying a nice set for a pretty price wasn't going to happen. So I prayed.

Sometimes God doesn't throw the new and best our way, but gives the old so we can create new. So there I stood, handing a dollar over with a happy heart for that ugly little table because God provided something I wanted. For me, it was perfect.

Leading two little boys into Home Depot for wood filler and spray paint finished off the morning, and both projects turned out beautifully. My husband had his shelf, and I had an end table on the porch beside the brown wicker love seat—which was also prayed for. Each time I looked at the four layers of brown paint I remembered the old chipped white, and was thankful, grateful to the Lord for providing it and giving us the ability to create beauty.

My sister is a master decorator. Because there are seven girls in our family, she receives lots of requests for advice on how to turn ugly into lovely.

I'm so glad she knows that her gift is God-given. That God is honored by her creating beauty as He is honored with her relationship with Him, and her mission work in South America. I honor her because she does all of it well, and each aspect turns her life into a lovely story.

Women love to sit at her table because she listens well, speaks truth, serves the hungry, and it's all done with her hand-crafted beauty around to touch the eyes as well as the soul.

When we know God, it all turns into worship.

Ladies, sisters, friends, let's not despise the small in search of the great. Jesus started small, in a stable, and didn't begin His ministry until age thirty. He asked fishermen to join Him, and ministered to cheaters and adulterers. He sat with sinners, and taught people on the seashore before climbing into a boat for rest—a *boat*, ladies, not a hotel or garden or home of His own.

For Him, too, it was all worship, and He was content.

I have to believe that every part of us is meant to be cultivated, enjoyed, and used in this world because God created this world and He needs beauty bringers just as He needs truth bearers. That my desire to create something out of nothing honors Him as well as something else one may do that seems more "spiritual."

Because when we are in Him, it all becomes a gift given right back to Him. And "we're not called because we're talented; we're talented because we're called." (Michael Tait, Newsboys*)*

He created all of it, and He wants all of it in return. Never despise the small when He's the One stirring desire in you. Never shut down your gift, your talent, when the Master Creator created you with it. Never go in search of another's when you already have your own.

Jesus didn't want the man with one talent to grasp for ten so he could be as good as his friend; Jesus wanted him to multiply what he was given.

But he hid it, instead. Buried it; ignored it. And his master came back, grieved, because he hadn't used what was given him. The other two had used and multiplied what they had been given whether it was five talents, or ten.

The amount really didn't matter; the use of it did. As JR VanProyen says, "We are accountable to God for what we do with the gifts we receive from God" (Kingsway Foursquare Church, sermon, Nov. 2017).

Live it all out with joy, because joy makes the world go round, and we need it all. *Everything God created is here because the world needs it. The world needs you. Simply cultivate well all you've been given!*

"Father, thank you that we don't need to strive for more than you've given us, but cultivate with joy all you've given."

DAY 91

"Show proper respect to everyone, love the family of believers, fear God, honor the emperor." 1 Peter 2:17, NIV

Honor is something you possess.

It is yours to give and is not controlled by others, which means you give it whether or not someone deserves it. You are a woman of honor, and *saints and sinners alike will benefit because of what you possess.*

Dishonoring someone discredits your own honor. *A woman of respect is honorable and shows strength of character regardless of those around her.* Dishonoring someone because of her own need only draws your own self down as well.

Honoring someone because they're like you can be selfish. It is easy to honor someone when you like what character qualities they possess, how financially savvy they are, or how fun they are to be around. It is easy to honor those who love what you love, think how you think, and do what you would do. Life, along with your worldview, changes when you honor all regardless of how much you agree with them.

Trying to change someone to become like us can be very dishonoring. If our spouse feels our dishonor, they may well go into survival mode to avoid facing more dishonor, and become crippled, unable to express themselves freely.

No one wants to be forced into a pseudo copy of another. When you accept someone for who they are, you show them honor, that they are worth as much as you are.

Honor includes seeking out the wonder of another. *Allow others to feel a boost when they interact with you.*

Christians often lack honor for others, which reveals a lack of seeing people as heaven sees them—people with a purpose and a God who longs to redeem them and make them new. Giving honor to all men is liberating and frees us to love even if we may regret their actions.

A heart full of honor is a heart full of joy. We see people with potential, purpose, and value.

The man who led our small group of worship team members was a great example. Some of us were young, some elderly, some had major life crises going on, and a few had quirks that annoyed the entire team. I had never seen someone so full of honor for everyone he met as that leader. He called out the best, the greatest gifts, by giving opportunity to those in whom he saw potential. Faults were addressed kindly, if at all, because his main goal was raising us up. When he had plenty of reason to criticize, he was silent.

Each week he wrote an email expressing thanks for our efforts and time. He greeted all of us and asked about peoples' welfare so much that I realized not enough time was spent talking about his own life.

The honor he showed all of us struck me. We could be young, insecure, have baggage, and still he saw the gift in us and called it out. We could have needs (and we did), and still he smiled and showed us honor.

When God did a personal thing, he called it forth in a group and had us share. But when needs were present, we often would not hear about them. We became a close, tightly knit group all because of one man's ability to honor others, and in that safe place, we opened up our deepest to each other.

I realized he wasn't looking for perfect people to join him in ministry, but real people. We began to meet weekly, while heart honesty and tears, joys, and victories were discussed among us. We felt safe, loved, and gave our best because he called out the best in us.

I saw our worship pastor bring life and vitality to dormant people. I heard many, many people talk of how much they loved and appreciated this man, and I never heard anything negative.

He could hang with skateboarders or lead worship with the team, chat over coffee or intercede for someone who needed it—all with a passion to grow another's heart because he possessed honor.

He didn't just save honor for those he felt deserved it, he readily handed it out because he was a man of honor; *he possessed it, and he saw people as Jesus did.*

A woman who sees her own purpose also values the purpose Christ created each person for, whether or not they are like her.

Live like this, and you will be a small part of bringing life into this world.

"Lord Jesus, help us pull the wonder—your wonder—
out of all those around us."

DAY 92

"Love is patient and kind; love does not envy or boast; it is not arrogant or rude. It does not insist on its own way; it is not irritable or resentful.

"It does not rejoice at wrong-doing, but rejoices with the truth.

"Love bears all things, believes all things, hopes all things, endures all things." 1 Corinthians 13:4–7, ESV

She sat there, a sobbing mass of humanity, vulnerable and broken. Was there risk in opening up her deepest heart? Absolutely. Was it pretty? Positively no.

The honor she was shown in the midst of her mess broke her even more, and an idea she had known all her life began to shape in her heart rather than her mind.

The idea that life is a story, God's story, and He's writing it each day. ***Somewhere in the center of the cross and the resurrection, the crown and the crucible, there has to be knowledge that both are part of His story.*** That if all of life was ease, we would be angels and not human, and if the trials we so want to avoid were omitted from our lives, we would be in heaven instead of earth.

It's just that we were born to love, to worship. In our deepest core, we were made to be a part of the redemptive side of humanity just like everyone else around us. We are not born craving relational difficulties or financial stress, loved ones passing away or pressure from those around us.

But life is real, not a fairy tale. It is dirty, not clean. It has valleys, sometimes very long, deep ones. We know this, but somehow suffering still takes us by surprise and we spin and we twirl and we gasp for air, and then, *we either learn to really live, or we slowly die while we live.*

We are not victims—we are victors—and we can't be victors without having a war to fight.

I watched her walk away with honor because she was given honor. I saw her heart soften and be even more vulnerable because in her time of need, she was treated with the love and honor every person craves when they are born. I watched her heart become lighter and her countenance clearer.

She chose to receive goodness and truth in the middle of her mess.

Something and someone grander, higher, nobler grabbed her attention and held it by reason of its greatness.

I saw what she saw—that life is too short to be wasted in grief over fallen humanity and their effects on one another; that each person is born with the right and capacity to love whether or not they are loved; *that honor is something we possess and grant to every soul because it's part of us whether or not it's part of them.*

A few minutes later I greeted an acquaintance. Sunshine splashed across the sky and seemed to call out the best and beautiful, but she sighed. She didn't feel well or lovely or capable of life in general. She was, in fact, beautiful (exceptionally so), and had a great number of wonderful experiences to boast of. But she was sighing.

I stood, fascinated with the story of it all. Struck by the wonder of honor and how we either possess it, or don't.

Honor allows you to walk through life with a certain triumph in your soul because you see how much God is worthy, and how much He honors you when you don't deserve it. *Honor allows you to view life and all those in it as born with a nature to love and be loved, to know redemption and healing.*

Honor allows you to step right in with God in His plan for people.

Honor allows you to encourage others and bring them to their highest potential.

Honor gives you freedom of soul to love on others without feeling threatened that your own honor is taken.

In short, honor allows you to see the way God sees — that we are all a part of the story He is writing and it is His story, not ours.

Honor brings incredible freedom. You get to give it no matter what, don't have to get bound up tightly because someone is not worthy of your honor. That friend who mistreated you is a person loved by God and He longs to bring them to redemption. It may be your own regard and honor (more than your disdain and disrespect) shown that brings them to see their need.

When our eyes open to see that the crucible — not just the crown — is part of His story in our lives, we begin to know the freedom in possessing honor.

"Father, thank you that you grab us by reason of your greatness; that there is meaning in the crucible and not only in the crown; that we can find peace in both."

DAY 93

"Love one another with brotherly affection. Outdo one another in showing honor." Romans 12:10, ESV

There's nothing like moving from a college town adjacent to another college town, with thousands of young folks walking the streets and filling cafés with backpacks and study books. The air is young. The vibes are youthful, fun, and vigorous.

Then we moved over the mountain pass onto the peninsula, where water is close and the air is temperate year-round, where you have mountains in the distance, sunny beaches close by, and wet winters instead of cold.

The result?

Hundreds of elderly couples move from California and other parts of the country to retire here. Coffeehouses are filled with gray heads bent over newspapers, having tea together, and perhaps even a budding romance between two elderly folk.

Parks are full of people walking their poodles. Dog shows happen where fuzzy little creatures perform stunts for retirees in their lawn chairs.

Cleaning jobs pay well because (some) elderly have resources and a generous heart.

Living with mature people surrounding us is a blessing.

Most of the time, that is, until you rush down the street only to be stuck behind twenty cars traveling below the speed limit because someone is driving ten miles below the speed limit.

I'm mothering and homeschooling four, have a law enforcement husband on various shifts, and run about constantly for one thing or another. Life is full to the max. I fume a bit inside as I crawl along the highway.

I join my husband at the gym and watch as various people walk into the treadmill area. I take a self-defense class with gray-headed men who used to be boxers and military men. One of them is more than past vigor and strength, but he's here. I look at my own husband, and yes, both men have the same inner drive to protect.

One is in his prime and the other has already been.

The elderly gentleman wants to be safe, too. For him, life is still important, and ill-minded men even more of a threat. I admire his ambition to defend himself, still.

Longer ago, the elderly were most honored. They had a place at their children's table and were cared for by family. Their advice was sought after and esteemed. They were loved, just as they loved the children who now ignore them in pursuit of their own lives. In today's culture, we forget that the elderly were once just like us—loving their kids with a passion and giving all they had to provide a good life for them. We grow up and ignore the very people who gave birth to us.

Women of honor know how to respect all. They can care for a mother when she's no longer able to care for herself because they know what she's already given.

Women of honor don't give honor only when it's easy to do so. Remember, *honor is something you possess because you are of honorable character.*

Women of honor find God's thoughts toward people of all ages, and implement a lifestyle of love toward all. They are compassionate and don't always take the easy way out.

They know how to honor even when the recipient may not be worthy of it.

In 2 Samuel 1 is the story of King David mourning the loss of his enemy and rival, King Saul. Prior to Saul's death he had tried, numerous times, to kill David. He was jealous, disobedient, and meant to keep the kingdom from becoming David's.

Saul's son, Jonathan, knew the kingdom would be given to David instead of himself, but still loved and supported him as his own brother. When Jonathan died in battle with his father, David said, "I am distressed for you, my brother Jonathan; you have been very pleasant to me; your love to me was wonderful, surpassing the love of women" (2 Samuel 1:26, NKJV).

Though he could not say the same of Saul, he says this of them both, "How have the mighty fallen, and the weapons of war perished!" (2 Samuel 1:27, NKJV)

One man deserved every ounce of David's respect and mourning; another man deserved none. Yet, because David knew that Saul had been the Lord's anointed, he mourned him when he died and refused to take arms against him when he lived. He had opportunity to kill Saul. He could have been joyful over his death.

David had more respect for the Lord's anointed than his own comfort and happiness.

In the same way, our respect for people God created with great potential should be obvious in all our lives. We don't hand it out freely only to those whom we think deserve it.

Possessing honor means you are loath to part with it in the way of showing dishonor. Knowing this changes our very lives.

We get to handle ourselves honorably rather than get pulled into dishonorable words or actions.

Women of purpose hold honor in highest value.

"Father, thank you for granting us the peace that comes from possessing honor and giving it to all. Thank you for the grace you show us when we are so far beneath you. Thank you for honoring us with your presence."

DAY 94

"Blessed are your eyes for they see, and your ears for they hear.

"I say to you that many prophets and righteous men desired to see what you see, and did not see it, and to hear what you hear, and did not hear it." Matthew 13:16–17, NKJV

Fall sunshine was disappearing into cold, the dog lay chewing on a brittle bone beside me, and my eyes pored over the words laying on the grass in front of me.

"The things you see . . . the things you hear . . ." (Matthew 13:17, NKJV).

My heart was wowed, because I knew I had seen it. I knew I had felt, tasted, experienced something those prophets I so admire wanted to know more of. They had to be speaking of this one thing I still can't find words for.

You know, those moments in life when you really feel like you can't go on. When the way is too rough, too steep, or that something makes you want to crawl into your bed and not get out again for a long time. When each passing minute makes you want to escape reality, like that day in January when my brother disappeared into murky waters, never to return.

We each have our own story. Life brings undeniable and often inescapable pain. To some, trials seem to last forever and you wonder why your story is written the way it is. Perhaps you face the loss of a child, lose a spouse, or lose your business.

None of us have Cinderella's magical godmother who turns life into pure bliss with a wave of her magic wand. We don't find our worn shoes turned into glass heels in one moment, nor do we go dancing down the hallway to enter the moment when we live happily ever after and all the deepest enemies of our joy are marched out of the kingdom, never to return.

Is this why grown women sit and cry over *Cinderella*?

But what is this mystery those prophets of old wanted to see?

Jesus says, "It has been given to you to know the mysteries of the kingdom of heaven . . ." (Matthew 13:11, NKJV).

I have to believe the secret He speaks about is this supernatural peace I got to have when the plane lifted me away from my brother's grave on foreign soil. I remember staring at the clouds and realized my heart felt as soft as they appeared.

I remember that year, holding on to that peace tenaciously when I wanted to go under. It was so powerful, so comforting, so life changing and life giving. I realized afresh that it really was "peace which surpasses all understanding" (Philippians 4:7, NKJV).

I saw, as never before, what a redeemer Jesus is. Not only for our sin, but for those things we don't know what to do with, and cannot escape. The waters rocked my boat, but the harder it rocked, the tighter He held.

Sometimes He allows the boat to rock so we see how tightly He is able to hold.

We don't see redemption until we need to be redeemed. Even the death of leaves in fall are making way for life in spring. So, when Christ breathed His last on the cross, He gave breath to His eternal presence in the hearts of all who believe.

The road to healing is never easy, but it is better than not walking at all. If you quit, you will be destroyed; if you keep walking, sooner or later you will see greener pastures and brighter skies.

God is all about healing. Whether your tragedy is external or internal, He is all about your well-being.

Believe this, and you will see His hand on your heart. Follow the road that's best, not easiest, and you will come to see better. Follow the easiest one, and you may well destroy your own self (which, by the way, no one else can do).

The life behind you is much less important than the future ahead of you. The key to inner well-being is the belief that no one else (and nothing else) can destroy what God has given you. He is for you, He wants you, He delights in you, He has great plans for you. He came for you, and is coming again one day to take you to Himself.

Walk with Him!

"Lord, thank you for being an inexhaustible mystery who brings meaning to the things in life we don't always understand."

DAY 95

---

*"Of this salvation the prophets have inquired and searched careful-
ly, who prophesied of the grace that would come to you, searching
what, or what manner of time, the Spirit of Christ who was in them
was indicating when He testified beforehand the sufferings of Christ
and the glories that would follow.*

*"To them it was revealed that, not to themselves, but to us they
were ministering the things which now have been reported to you
through those who have preached the gospel to you by the Holy Spirit sent from heaven—things which angels desire to look into." 1 Peter
1:10–12, NKJV*

Because God is the definition of love, and we were created
in His image, we have deep capacity for love. The desire to
be adored is there because we were *meant to be adored.* Even a
baby knows when something is wrong in its environment.

Did you know you can test a baby's urine to find out how
much the parents fight?

There are two kinds of emotional pain; one is the severe
kind, such as rejection, abuse, or betrayal, and the other is considered less severe, but in reality can do much damage. This is
the lack of positive input such as care, love, and encouragement. Believe it or not, these can be similar in effect.

Then there is grief in its rawest form, such as when you lose a loved one. We are born to be surrounded with our loved ones, not to lose them.

If these words strike a chord in your heart, listen in carefully.

Trauma is anything that causes the well-being of your heart to drain faster than it can fill up with love and joy. Picture with me a bucket with a hole in the bottom, draining water faster than a trickle pours into the top. So we, though we may have good in our lives, will still be empty unless the hole is fixed, the pain is healed.

The good news is that we don't have a right to stay wounded; we have a right to be healed.

An empty bucket with a hole in the bottom becomes useless. When we cannot put a stop to the pain draining our hearts, we become less than useful. Hurting people generally hurt people. In one way or another, when we are devoid of life and vitality, we become a burden to those around us. We may even lash out in fear, anger, or abusive words and behavior.

Hurt people often wait around for something to change. When this doesn't happen, they live, sometimes for years, carrying the pain of grief or offense. This does a lot of damage because we were created for something better.

Though our needs are expressed differently than a child's, adults need healing no less. We are not some superhuman with no feelings who can handle anything because somehow we are "strong." The hurts in our lives are not meant for us to carry; we are affected, plain and simple. And if not healed, pain has a way of draining the good from our minds, hearts, and emotions.

We cannot just manage pain; we must allow ourselves to be healed, or grief will define us.

If you are one with a hole draining more than what's pouring in, you need answers. It is not OK to keep going on without help. Your heart literally craves healing as much or more than your body craves food.

We tend to cover our pain while trying to ease our hearts with other things.

If we are successful, we will feel better, we think. Or we try to find meaning in pursuing a hobby or relief by indulging in food. We may pursue some long-forgotten dream, but false intimacy never fulfills your desire for true intimacy with Christ, and no dream, hobby, or food will ever heal pain of heart.

As Mike Van Proyen says, "Jesus doesn't stand back and speak on third person; Jesus gets personal" (Sunday morning sermon, KingsWay Foursquare Church, Nov. 2017).

Our world is geared toward conditional love. People are conditional; we tend to love the lovable. We may shy away from a grieving person, may avoid a hurting one. But God loves us in our ugliest, messiest mess, when our eyes are still full of tears.

Part of healing pain comes from believing in and receiving His love right in the middle of our grief.

We will never work our way out. We must simply position ourselves to receive the love Christ offers, and as it washes over our souls, we will be changed from the inside.

He wins us with love. He heals us with love.

Sometimes, things don't change and your place remains draining enough to burn a new hole in your bucket all over again. Sometimes, loss remains for the rest of your days. When you lose a loved one, no amount of tears will bring them back. My brother will never return to this earth no matter how great the hole in our family is.

If your situation cannot change, God offers healing more complete than anyone else can. You are not destined to waste away. It is your birthright, as a child of God, to be healed regardless of whether or not your situation changes.

If you trust Him, He will find you and hold you closer than any human could. He will come in and give you peace. He will comfort you right in the middle of your mess with a comfort greater than human love could offer. *He will, in fact, make your life richer with love than many experience who have never needed to cling to the Source of true comfort like you have.*

It is your birthright to be healed because your God is a healer. It is your right to experience love because He is love and He is your Father.

It is your right to have a heart filled with His goodness because He is good, and *no earthly person or thing can stop the flow of His goodness right into your heart if you are brave enough to open the door.*

"Lord, open our hearts to receive your inclusive goodness in the face of impossible odds."

DAY 96

"And from His fullness we have all received, grace upon grace.
"For the law was given through Moses; grace and truth came through Jesus Christ." John 1:16–17, ESV

Her heart shook, trembled as she knelt on the hard floor. "God, I don't know what to do with this one."

No matter how hard she tried, there didn't seem to be a way out of the intense pain of heart. Few understood, could understand. And even if they did, who could help? Some things are too deep, too complicated for people to solve. Some things only Christ can speak to, bring relief from, and heal. Some things, like a loved one's death, never change.

Her heart squeezed tightly and felt as if it would forever stay squeezed. The floor was hard under her knees, but she stayed, thirsty for a God touch. Days of searching for answers had brought nothing but more intensity.

Somehow in her mind's eye she saw it; a strong arm reaching down, hand extended, finger out for her to grasp. She heard it, a still, small voice assuring her that He was there to hold tightly. That if she trusted, she would find peace regardless of how she felt today.

She gritted her teeth and said yes. She saw the finger reaching down, and she reached up.

That was it, and that was all she could do.

Does this story sound familiar? The more women I meet, the more I know the silent struggle, the heartache, the unspoken cry of heart. To greater or lesser degrees, we can all relate.

And it is here that God meets us, right at the end, when we cry like a child, feel like a child, and life's weight weighs heavily on our shoulders. When we find no answers, see no light, and all we can do is keep stumbling along. When mist falls on the windows of our hearts, and to survive, we try to quash our feelings.

Here, right here, is where the arm reaches down, the hand is extended, and help comes to the heart. When the world goes quiet, and no sound is heard but the groan of your heart.

When you take His hand and whisper, "I'm yours, and you have me," new life forms within you and a richness of soul emerges in your heart that you could not otherwise know.

Your darkest hour will bring your brightest light.

For, would you really hang on that tightly in your sunny days? Would you even see the arm extended and mercy holding you? But when we are taken down and swallowed under and we can't breathe and the tunnel doesn't have a light at the end, we hang on and He hangs on, and our soul merges into His because it has nowhere else to go.

He has you. He holds you. No matter what.

You are loved. You will be strong. You will survive, and then, you will thrive. All because He is, and He is stronger than what has gotten you, and when you are in Him, you are also stronger than what has gotten you.

You are loved. You are His.

Rest well, daughter. *You were destined for glory, and when your resources are gone and there is nothing else to do but let it go, you will find it. You are redeemed.*

And that means *no matter what*.

> *"Father, thank you for redemption. You allow us to fall, but catch us before we crash. Thank you for holding us."*

DAY 97

"But those who wait on the Lord shall renew their strength; they shall mount up with wings like eagles; they shall run and not be weary, they shall walk and not faint." Isaiah 40:31, NKJV

We may measure Him by what we experience, but God is immeasurable.

Can we trust Him? Absolutely yes!

Because we understand? No, but because He does. Because we live with strength He gave, from breath He put into our body, which He planned and tenderly formed in the womb before we could even think.

To trust in such a God is an honor.

Seeing Him as transcending all things brings us to this place of being held when our hearts break, of seeing grief as drawing us into worship, of finding deepest comfort in our greatest pain. Worship is not so much something we do, as it is a state of the heart.

The world is longing, hungry, desperate for answers in a sin-wrecked world. When we look up, we find relief because God is all about redemption and healing, and His goodness is not comparable to earth's brokenness.

Meaning is so much greater than matter; meaning is

knowing the Master. It's as if we run in circles with our own feelings, and all the while God is calling us to return to the one basic thing we need—Himself! As we see Him higher than tragedy and more magnificent than all beauty combined, we begin to feel His fullness right where we are.

From a place of fullness, we are able to bring beauty into our world.

We dare to live fully even though nothing changes in our circumstance. And then, we get to experience the beauty our hearts long for.

Sometimes I wake, and my heart seems to gasp for breath. I can see my brother in my mind's eye, going down eighty feet of watery depths. The vivid picture sears into my mind in those first few thoughts of the day. Images no one ever wants to imagine with loss no one expects. I fight to gain control.

How many of you wake with searing reminders of the problem in your life? You gasp for breath, for enough strength to face the day. Your feet hit the floor unwillingly because at least in sleep you forget this daunting reality you cannot escape.

Did you know that eagles are the only bird who, when the need rises, can stare straight into the sun and fly toward it? Eyes protected with a thin layer of God-created film, they soar away from whatever tries to destroy them, straight toward the sun.

When your heart mounts away and above toward the Son, you know in greater measure how good God is. *If the trial is absent we don't need wings.* Soaring is always exhilarating—soaring above whatever grabs at the core of your being brings you to a new reality of redemption.

So let come what may, in the name of the Son of God, we triumph. We do more than survive, we thrive. It's our gift, our heritage, and what *makes belief in the Son become the most precious thing we will ever experience.*

"Father, today give us the strength to rise, to soar, to fly."

Day 98

"Therefore choose life, that both you and your descendants may live." Deuteronomy 30:19b, NKJV

My feet pounded on the pavement and my heart pounded just as hard. I tossed my head and wondered for the hundredth time why health and exercise don't come easy. No matter what form of exercise I choose, it takes more push than I naturally want to give.

CrossFit was grueling. Running, then lifting, then running, then lifting. Or running, then climbing rope when my legs were already weak and shaky. A regular gym isn't much better. I can't grow muscle without stretching my limits in strength. Working out at home takes push as well, or little gets accomplished.

As the sun beat on my face, I saw a parallel. Exercising faith is hard work. It takes push. A whole lot of courage. Sometimes we pray hard and lean hard and breathe hard until we are able to trust well.

It's a whole lot easier to quit. You know, go down in depression when your brother passes away or you face sudden illness. But we hear that still, small whisper that there's good in store if we keep loving and allow God to bring good into the ugly.

Years down the road we either have victories gained, or reminders of what could have been.

Faith is God's word and will when our own way seems so much easier. But in the end, is our own way better? Not at all. Oh, the blessings we miss, the trials we bring onto ourselves by not listening in faith to God's *good word*. Ours may seem easier, but God's is perfect.

Jesus untwists the lies of our own ways with faith in, and wholehearted submission to, our Father's will.

Three times, Jesus cried out, Saying, "Father, if it is Your will, take this cup away from me; nevertheless not My will, but yours be done" (Luke 22:42, NKJV).

Jesus, God's Son, wanted *out*.

What do you want out of?

Jesus's Father told him no, and led Him straight into the dark abyss of human suffering and sin. Sweat rolled like drops of blood while he fervently asked for a way out, but instead, He was led through. Right through the deepest, darkest cesspool of pain and bearing sin—not his own—that He could imagine.

He felt forsaken, and asked God why He was left alone.

But He wasn't. His Father was right there, close, never leaving, and granting grace. He allowed those nails to pound straight through. He heard the sneers of the people He came to save, who now thought they won. He embraced the dark awfulness of sin.

He bore the burden of our despicable treachery and died a death unknown to the realm of His Godhead. *He embraced us. They embraced us. They were both there through it all.*

But in His dying, he destroyed death. In bearing our sin, He triumphed over it. In allowing God to have His way, He became Victor once again. In listening when He wanted to run, He entered rest and reigned triumphant.

Had He chosen His own way out, He would still be in the very darkness He was wanting to escape.

So we, when we follow hard, find a way out. Because we can turn from God, or we can turn to God.

What is God saying to you in the trial you want to escape? As opposite from your own desires or comfort it may be, follow it, and you will be blessed. In doing so, you will thwart whatever plan there was to bring you down with a wholehearted embrace to the Father's word to you.

There is always a good word to follow that will lead us upward.

"Father, help us to know that you never keep us in something without leading us into something good. That in our death, life springs forth; that the very thing meant to harm us is the thing that will lead us into more of you."

Day 99

"Walk in obedience to all that the Lord your God has commanded you; so that you may live and prosper and prolong your days in the land that you will possess." Deuteronomy 5:33, NIV

The sun shone hot, and I tore another smelly bag open. If anything makes me question America's lifestyle, it's a trip to the recycling plant.

The son had tied, no, knotted those gigantic black bags shut. And I muttered under my breath, "I've told him a hundred times."

Trying to pull those knots out makes the job so much more difficult. And so does having plastic and cardboard in the same bag. My hands got sticky, and I griped about the fact that I had asked him not to tie those tight knots and not to mix the recyclables—like a hundred times.

A few faces were smiling as they milled about the great green bins, but I was not. I was on my way to the orthopedic surgeon with the littlest, and I wanted to be clean, but here I was, sticky with old yuck.

"I've told him a hundred times."

It hit me with a jolt. God must feel this way about me, about us, when we do the same old things over, and over, and over. Like me, with fear and insecurities. I'd been hounded that very morning with the same old fear that grabbed at me, pushed its way into the fiber of my being where all I wanted to do was crash into a muddle of insecurities.

How many times does God have to whisper the same thing to me? How many times do I have to hear Him say, "I have this. I have *you*."

Our humanity was never meant to compete with God's perfection. When we embrace our weakness, His strength is perfected in it.

How long do we need the same lesson, and how long will our lives be dotted with the same instances? Because really, He promises peace. He gives rest. He holds us, and when we allow ourselves to be held, He holds so tightly that nothing can get to us. *Nothing.*

Today, we can dare reach out and be held. We must. Today we can walk in peace. And sooner or later, *one day after another of being held leads to a lifetime, and we look back with awe that we found deliverance from the things that grabbed our core so strongly.*

Today, dare with me to place your faith in the One who longs to hold you.

"Father, at the end of the day and the end of life, when eternity begins and we enter your presence, our questions won't matter as much as our trust in you, who knows all things. Help us follow hard when you speak."

DAY 100

"For Thou hast possessed my reins: You have covered me in my mother's womb. I will praise you, for I am fearfully and wonderfully made: marvelous are your works, and that my soul knows right well.

"My substance was not hid from you, when I was made in secret, and curiously wrought in the lowest parts of the earth.

"Your eyes did see my substance, yet being imperfect; and in your book all my members were written, which in continuance were fashioned, when as yet there was none of them.

"How precious also are your thoughts unto me, O God! How great is the sum of them!" Psalm 139:13–17, ESV

She brushed it on with an inner sigh. That gooey black stuff everyone expects you to swipe on your delicate lashes to make them look fuller, thicker, longer.

It was a busy morning when a hundred other things called for her attention. And so often, as she stood in front of the mirror brushing on the mascara, her youngest yelled in the living room.

Lora got to thinking. Why the pressure each day? Was *she* really this insecure? What was wrong with going about in her own skin?

One day she felt the tug. "Don't wear makeup today. Show your daughters that value is not based on outer beauty."

Outer beauty should never define who we are.

I know several lovely teen girls who stay clear of makeup most days. One of them told me she didn't want her man to get used to her in a brushed-up state, only to be disappointed when he sees her in her real self after marriage. This girl has some sense and will never be one of those wives who run to the bathroom to apply the brush before her husband wakes up.

Your friends want real. They want you more than your beauty, and if beautifying yourself is stressing you out, let the brush drop, put away that curling iron, and relax.

If you can't do that around your friends, you are probably hanging with the wrong crowd. Find yourself some honest-to-goodness friends who love you for you.

By all means, figure this out when you're young, or you will fight age like some overworked shrew squinting at the screen for beauty products to help conceal the fact that you're just like everyone else—you're getting older.

God never asks us to stay young—He asks us to become wiser with each passing year.

I have some awesome friends. Some of them fast from certain things during the first of the year, including food, coffee, Facebook, or other things. One day my friend came to church services with no makeup on her face, and she shared with me how the Lord prompted her to lay it aside for a while. Then she laughed as she recalled certain people asking her if she felt ill, and her reply to them, "No, I feel great!"

My friend has long been an example of confidence and joy. She's a beautiful person in every way, and I admire her obedience and boldness to take down one of her security props. And even more, her words, *"I dare not think thoughts about myself that God doesn't think."*

Colbie Caillat was one brave, daring singer when she wrote "You Don't Have to Try So Hard." She walked into the studio one day, upset about the pressure to live up to expectations in both image and music. She defied it all with her song, when, in front of the camera, she peeled off those long gorgeous lashes, wiped off all her eye makeup, and stood there, bare for the world to see. Her video got over 55,000,000 views and thousands of likes.

She was beautiful in her bare skin, but it was a different, natural beauty made stark by her bravery to show the difference. I honor this girl who is used to cameras flashing all over her gorgeously done-up face, hair, and body. I honor her for letting the world know she is Photoshopped on some of her album covers, as are most other artists. I honor her for posting photos of her real self and saying, "It felt really cool to be in front of the camera with no makeup on."

From her platform of popularity she shows us that outer beauty is not our most important asset—being comfortable with ourselves is even more beautiful.

Who in the world are we, anyway?

We look at everyone around us and wonder where in the world we fit. What is our worth? Who, and what, in all this world, should we measure ourselves by?

This world holds much pressure. People judge each other by the clothes they wear, the jobs they have, how clean their houses are, how beautiful they are, and by how many and what kind of friends they have. Mrs. Smith meets Mrs. Jones and immediately a subconscious analysis takes place. She leaves, having "clicked" with the lady she met, having decided her too far beneath or above her status, or having felt intimidated by some quality Mrs. Jones possessed that she did not. Both Mrs. Smith and Mrs. Jones and many other ladies out there feel the daily pressure of their worth being measured by outward appearance and things.

Women tend to walk into a room full of people with their greatest concern being what kind of impression they will make—not how they can most bless those they meet. And somewhere, deep inside, they long to be free from the fear of being judged by others.

When we meet a person who is original, has no airs, and loves everyone regardless of status or perfection, we are drawn immediately. When we realize that our worth is not measured by what people think, and accept ourselves for who God made us to be, our hearts come alive.

Instead of feeling bound up with intimidation, we relax and our true selves shine forth, for deep inside we know our true value to a great and good Creator God.

It really doesn't matter who the world thinks we are; the world's standards change. And, the very people who judge by outward things are themselves fearful of being judged by people just like you. It's a vicious cycle, designed by the devil to keep people in bondage. The more people refuse to play the game, the more freedom we will all experience.

In her book *The True Measure of a Woman*, Lisa Bevere writes, "Part of being beautiful and authentic is realizing the value of you, the original! An original is the beginning of something. You were never meant to be defined by others and reduced to a pseudo copy or forgery. Do you know there is something extremely unique and beautiful only you have? Whether you embrace your uniqueness or live out your life as only a mixed

THE MASTER CAT